The Silent Garden

The Silent Garden

Understanding the Hearing Impaired Child

Paul W. Ogden, Ph.D., & Suzanne Lipsett

Contemporary Books, Inc.
Chicago

Library of Congress Cataloging in Publication Data

Ogden, Paul W.
  The silent garden.

  Reprint. Originally published: 1st ed. New York: St. Martin's Press, c1982.
  Includes index.
  1. Children, Deaf—Family relationships.
2. Deaf—Education.   I. Lipsett, Suzanne.   II. Title.
HV2392.2.O34   1983   362.8'2   82-22142
ISBN 0-8029-5571-5

Design by Dennis J. Grastorf

Published by Contemporary Books, Inc.
180 North Michigan Avenue, Chicago, Illinois 60601
Manufactured in the United States of America
Library of Congress Catalog Card Number: 82-22142
International Standard Book Number: 0-8092-5571-5

Published simultaneously in Canada by
Beaverbooks, Ltd.
150 Lesmill Road
Don Mills, Ontario M3B 2T5
Canada

This edition published by
arrangement with St. Martin's Press.

This book is dedicated to
Dorothy C. Ogden, Paul's very special mother,
who cherishes the following poem:

HEAVEN'S VERY SPECIAL CHILD

A meeting was held quite far from Earth.
"It's time again for another birth,"
Said the angels to the Lord above.
"This special child will need much love.
His progress may seem very slow,
Accomplishments he may not show
And he'll require extra care
From the folks he meets way down there.
He may not run or laugh or play;
His thoughts may seem quite far away.
In many ways he won't adapt,
And he'll be known as handicapped.
So let's be careful where he's sent,
We want his life to be content.

Please, Lord, find parents who
Will do a special job for you.
They will not realize right away
The leading role they're asked to play
But with this child sent from above
Comes stronger faith and richer love.
And soon they'll know the privilege given
In caring for this gift from Heaven.
Their precious charge, so meek and mild
Is Heaven's very special child."

—Author Unknown

and to Suzanne's father, Mitchell Lipsett, a rock.

Table of Contents

The Silent Garden

Preface

DEAFNESS AFFECTS COMMUNICATION, perhaps the most complex human activity. Therefore, it is different from other disabilities and much more difficult to understand. The purpose of this book is to introduce to people who need most to understand deafness the implications of hearing impairment for communication, learning, and simply living among other people, both hearing and deaf. Because deafness is widely misunderstood even by those closest to it, we felt in writing this book that our most urgent task was to reach the parents of children newly discovered to be deaf. Therefore, the book addresses parents directly. Our overall intention, however, is to reach all people who live with, work with, or want to know better a deaf child or deaf children. This extended audience includes siblings, relatives, friends, and loved ones as well as teachers, other school personnel, and those who encounter deaf children in social and recreational work. Federally mandated mainstreaming of disabled children into the public schools has brought deaf children into contact with many people who have had no preparation for understanding deafness and its profound implications for living and learning. It is our hope that this book will reach these people and serve them as a bridge to the world of deafness.

1

Hearing loss occurs on a spectrum from mild through moderate and severe to profound. Within these terms, this book is concerned with children who are considered severely to profoundly deaf and who are either born so or become so before they learn to speak or understand language. Another way of classifying hearing loss is to say that people who are totally incapable of understanding speech through the ear, whether with or without a hearing aid, are called *deaf,* and those with a hearing loss that allows some understanding of speech through the aided or unaided ear are termed *hard of hearing.* Under these definitions, our subject is the deaf rather than the hard-of-hearing child, although parents, teachers, friends, and associates of hard-of-hearing children will also benefit from the material discussed here.

Finally, we must begin our exploration of the deaf child's world with a cautionary note. Although a significant number of deaf children fall into the category of the multiply handicapped, multiple handicaps and their effects lie outside the scope of this book. Rather, our intention is to familiarize readers with deafness alone. We believe that parents of all deaf children, regardless of other factors, can benefit from an increased understanding of deafness. However, we urge parents of children with multiple disabilities to look to qualified specialists for help in understanding their children's particular needs.

Our warmest thanks go to the many people who helped us in our work on this book: Karen Jensen, Jean Ching, Catie Freer, Bette Baldis, Nancy Mitchell, Susan Wengraf, Katy Ray, Dorcas Kessler, Liz Montague, Nancy Bartholomew, Betty McAfee, Danny Moses, Diana Landau, and Rosalie Bergmann.

Special appreciation goes to Beryl Leiff Benderly for her admirable book *Dancing Without Music.* And affectionate thanks go to our families—Anne Keenan Ogden, Dunbar H. Ogden III, Annegret Ogden, Tom Rider, Samuel Rider, Mitchell Lipsett, and Adele Lipsett—for their enthusiasm for our project and their cheerful encouragement.

Introduction

GREGORY AND ELIZABETH are a young couple with three children aged thirteen months, two years, and four years. Until recently, their family life seemed ideal. However, at age ten months, their baby Ginny was diagnosed as profoundly deaf from birth. Gregory and Elizabeth were stunned. Overnight, their contented family was shattered by anxiety and bewilderment. Almost as devastating as Ginny's diagnosis was Elizabeth's reaction to it, a deep, seemingly incurable depression. For the three months since the diagnosis, Elizabeth has been barely able to go through the motions of daily life. All her children, not just Ginny, are in need of her attention and are beginning to worry about her. Gregory is starting to resent her inability to come to grips with reality. And Elizabeth herself is burdened by guilt, for she feels incapable of making the effort to find out how she can help Ginny. She is haunted by a feeling of loss. The little girl she thought she knew is gone—in fact never existed at all. For Elizabeth, it is as if Ginny had died, only to be replaced by a demanding and troublesome stranger.

*   *   *

Andrew, age eight, lost his hearing as a result of meningitis when he was three months old. Almost as soon as deafness was confirmed, Andrew's parents, Barbara and John, began to research the options open to their son. Very soon they met an audiologist who encouraged them to put their faith in education and to concentrate their efforts on teaching Andrew to speak. They sent Andrew to a speech-oriented preschool for deaf children and when he was six years old enrolled him in a residential oral school in a neighboring state. The family had a modest income, but they risked what security they had to buy a house near Andrew's school. However, despite his parents' efforts and their considerable financial investment, Andrew was slow to learn speech and is not showing an aptitude for reading lips. After two years at the school, his language comprehension and reading skills are developing, but so far verbal conversation has eluded him. Worse than his speech difficulty is the fact that Andrew and his parents have no means of getting through to each other; he learned sign language, but John and Barbara never did. Therefore, Andrew is often shut out from family life by his deafness. His main frustration lies in trying to figure out what is going on in the hearing world and get his messages across to others, and it causes him many moments of fury each day. His parents sympathized with his temper tantrums when he was younger, but they expected them to abate as he grew older. Instead, Andrew's anger at being cut off from others seems to grow each year. The atmosphere within the family crackles with tension, and both parents are in the habit, figuratively, of walking on tiptoe for fear of eliciting Andrew's rage. The thought of Andrew's approaching adolescence sends his parents into despair.

* * *

Ted is a telephone-line repairman whose wife died three years ago, leaving him with two young children. Ted works days and as much overtime as he can to support his family, and he depends on a housekeeper to look after the children. In the three years since his wife's death, four housekeepers have come and gone. All four cited little Caroline as their reason for leaving—she was "impossible," they said, hard to discipline, and "Well—perhaps a little slow?" At age two, Caroline was discovered to be severely deaf, probably because of the birth complications that resulted in her mother's death. At the time of the diagnosis, both Caroline and her brother Jordy started showing signs of emotional disturbance. Both were sullen and withdrawn and refused to eat their meals.

When Ted learned that Caroline was deaf, he barely comprehended the meaning of the problem. He had never known any deaf people and had no idea what could be done for Caroline. He went to doctor appointments with her when he could, but he was already in danger of losing his job because of time he missed in interviewing housekeepers. Therefore, Caroline was taken to the doctor by the housekeeper, whose reports to Ted were vague at best. As to what services exist for deaf people in his community, Ted is still totally uninformed. In fact, he is unaware of the fact that deaf people can learn to communicate and live productive, independent lives. Owing to his total ignorance of the subject, Ted associates deafness with brain damage. His only goal is to obtain reliable child care for Caroline and her brother, and he has resigned himself to the notion that Caroline will remain at home under care for the rest of her life.

*   *   *

These sketches depict classic situations that may arise in families of deaf children. Such problems occur no matter how well intentioned a deaf child's parents may be—and no matter how well educated, how sophisticated, or how rich. Problems develop because deafness is a serious disability affecting communication. Because our culture values verbal, speech-oriented communication above all other forms, deaf people are at a severe disadvantage. Very often, deafness occurs in people who have other disabilities as well, making a tough situation that much harder. In short, deafness always brings difficulties, not only for hearing-impaired people but for their families as well.

The parents of a deaf child invariably feel their child's frustrations and disappointments, but at the same time they have special problems of their own. How do you help a hearing-impaired child communicate? What school should you choose? How do you deal with the effects of the disability on other children in the family? Above all, how do you maintain your faith in your own common sense in the face of conflicting but convincing professional advice? For parents attempting to raise independent, productive, well-adjusted individuals, deafness in a child can mean a decades-long balancing act on the outer edges of patience and hope.

But having faced the reality of their child's deafness, parents can begin to steer a zigzag course around the obstacles encountered by the deaf and those who love them. A family may move through one bad patch only to see another troublespot looming ahead. But parents can feel their progress as their deaf children gain confidence and mastery over the environment.

This book does not offer easy solutions to the difficult problems of raising deaf children. Nor does it attempt to convince you of the merit of this or that method of communication, this or that technique of counseling or schooling. Rather, the book demonstrates that, *whatever the communication method or schooling strategy you choose for your child,* his or her deafness need not stand in the way of a rich family life. Nor does deafness block your child's chances for a satisfying, independent adulthood. While always acknowledging the seriousness of the disability, the book asserts that parents who learn to trust their own common sense and their children's desire to learn and adapt can go a long way toward helping their children compensate for their deafness.

Simply stated, the purpose of this book is to aid parents, family members, and interested professionals in viewing prelingually deaf children (children who are born deaf or who become deaf before acquiring language capability) not as "poor deaf people," whose main characteristic is their deafness, but as whole human beings who happen to be deaf. The basic idea is to remind the reader that although deaf children have difficulty communicating, their need and desire to communicate are as great as those of hearing children of the same age. And although the hearing of deaf children is impaired, their brains, their eyes, their voices, their hands, their whole bodies, are still capable of conveying and receiving information.

The concept of the whole child might seem overly simple to some. But for one hundred years the field of deaf education has been marked by controversy and debate regarding the best modes of communication for the deaf. As the conflict waxed and waned and scholarly journal vied with journal, the notion of the whole child, as opposed to the deaf child, often got lost in the fray. Educators, therapists, and parents alike often became so intent on furthering their favorite method of communication—whether signing, fingerspelling, speech- and lipreading, or total communication—that the importance of a healthy home environment, parents' intuition, social stimulation, nonverbal communication, playfulness, open affection, humor, honest anger, and old-fashioned fair-mindedness tended to be minimized or ignored. This book focuses on all these aspects of family life. It attempts to sidestep the controversies and give due consideration to the value of common sense. In doing so, the book sets itself apart from other works on the special needs of deaf children.

A second factor distinguishes this book even more sharply. Most books on deafness are written by hearing professionals in the fields of deaf education or the psychology of deafness. But although this book was cowritten by a hearing writer, the primary author is himself deaf, profoundly and from birth. All the material found here is based on Paul Ogden's experiences, his interviews with two hundred parents of deaf children, and his discussions, both formal and informal, with more than two hundred fifty deaf people. The experience and knowledge of

other writers and researchers are by no means devalued here—
Paul Ogden himself is associate professor of communicative
disorders at California State University at Fresno and a re-
searcher in the fields of deafness and deaf education. But the
personal experiences of the author and his informants lend a
perspective on deafness until now unavailable to hearing parents of deaf children.

We do not dismiss the importance of professional expertise
and guidance. Clearly, all the parents described in the opening
sketches needed professional help in moving out of the stale-
mates they had reached. Deafness has complex and subtle effects on a child's abilities to communicate and to interact with
others. The teaching of sophisticated forms of communication
and the resolution of interpersonal difficulties require the skill
and knowledge that only highly trained professionals possess.
Thus, in addition to exploring a child's family, the world of
nonverbal communication, and methods for engendering self-
reliance and self-esteem, this book surveys thoroughly all
available options regarding communication methods, education strategies, telecommunication aids, and services.

The resources available are described in a nonpartisan way,
free from the controversies they have generated in the past. It
is our view that each child and each family is unique and that
no one program is best for everyone. Decisions on what communication method to stress, what kind of school to choose,
what type of counseling, if any, is called for, are personal matters. Doubtless these are among the most difficult decisions
parents will ever make. Nevertheless, a book can only provide
the relevant information; it cannot make decisions. It is our
hope that the information here will help to make parents'
choices well informed.

To summarize, this book offers a holistic approach to raising deaf children, based on common sense and sound scientific
knowledge. By *holistic* we mean that we focus attention on the
whole child—not the brain, the mouth, the communication
skills, social skills, or emotions of the child, but the whole per-

son, including his or her potential as an adult. But the concept extends even further: it encompasses you as parents as well. Parenting is not something you do *to* your child; it is an experience you enter into *with* your child. This book describes a way of enriching that experience for both parent and child as fully as possible. By strengthening your relationship with your deaf child, both of you will profit as you enter the obstacle course before you.

Chapter 1

What to Expect . . .
From Yourself

YOU MIGHT BE SURPRISED to find a book about deaf children beginning with a chapter directed only to parents. After all, isn't your child your first concern as a parent? And now that you have learned your child is deaf, shouldn't you be making up for the time lost before the problem was discovered?

Yes, a deaf child needs special help and attention. There is no question that the sooner you learn what your own child needs and provide it, the sooner he or she will learn to communicate despite the hearing impairment. But as the parent of a child with a significant disability *you* have special needs as well. In many ways, this book is as much about you as about your child. As an adult and a parent, you will make decisions on how your child will communicate, the school your child will attend, the extent of therapy and other professional help your child will receive, and the kind of hearing aid your child will use. These decisions will strongly affect the child all through life—socially, emotionally, and intellectually.

To make these decisions and take these actions, you will have to be clearheaded, emotionally stable, and physically hardy. You might have to extend yourself further than you ever have before. To do so, your first need is to absorb the new knowledge that has shaken you so deeply: your child is deaf. The time directly following confirmation of this fact is *your* time. For the child who has been deaf from birth or for a significant period following a disease, nothing has altered. For you, life has changed irrevocably.

THE RESPONSE CYCLE

Each child is different; each parent is, too. Further, levels of deafness differ from person to person. The combinations of personalities, potentials, family structure, and social and economic factors that, along with deafness, shape a deaf person's situation are infinite. Just as varied are the reactions of individual parents to the knowledge that their children's hearing is impaired.

Still, in recent years it has been confirmed that people reacting to crises in their lives go through a series of responses that are common to everyone. The stages in the cycle, though expressed differently in different people, are basically the same. The cycle is composed of five stages, termed *shock, recognition, denial, acknowledgment,* and *constructive action.* The response cycle begins when a person learns of an inescapable fact that will make life more difficult. The cycle is completed when the individual fully accepts the new conditions of life and takes action to adapt to them. The response cycle seems to be built into our psyches to enable us to react gradually to unexpected changes.

The response cycle is natural in times of crisis. Conversely, an interruption in the cycle is unnatural and unhealthy. The chief danger for a person faced with a serious but inescapable life change is that he or she might get stuck at some point in the response cycle—becoming mired in, say grief or self-pity rather than feeling these emotions and then moving on. The purpose of this chapter is to help you guard against becoming trapped at a particular stage. The best way to avoid this pitfall is to be aware of the cycle and to learn to recognize where you are within it.

As you progress through the cycle after learning of your

child's deafness, you will be battered many times by intense and painful emotions. At these times it may help you to know where you are in the response cycle and to recognize that your feelings are natural, useful, and above all necessary. Let yourself feel everything that comes to you. Do not be frightened or disgusted by the strength of your feelings or the forms they take. Do not deny your feelings; allow them to come. Do not try to change them; you will never succeed.

In some ways the response cycle is a cleansing process. Simply knowing that you are in the midst of the cycle will help you. Furthermore, you will find comfort in the fact that what you go through has been experienced by others in your situation. You can be sure that, like others before you, you will move through the more painful stages into a position of strength. At that point you will think more clearly and perhaps act more effectively than you ever did before.

The sections that follow treat each phase of the response cycle in turn. But before moving on to these more detailed descriptions, it is important to mention that for the family of a deaf child the cycle of response is not a one-time experience. The cycle recurs time and again as the child matures and faces new challenges. For families of all children, disabled or not, each stage of life—beginning school, starting adolescence, entering young adulthood—holds new difficulties. But for the hearing-impaired child, the rites of passage pose special problems. At each of these times when life's difficulties loom larger for your child, you are likely to go through the response cycle once more, though the intensity of your responses may vary. If you know what to expect from yourself, you will be far ahead of the game, for you will be able to look to past experience for guidance. Also, you can be confident that you will eventually emerge from your shock and dismay with a clearer understanding of the difficulty you and your child face together.

Shock

The first reaction to devastating news is shock. This response, which lasts from a few hours to a few days at most, is a stunned calm in which the mere truth of the situation is absorbed apart from its implications. Typically, parents report something like "The audiologist told me my child was deaf but it didn't really sink in." Shock is a protective device that enables you to take in bad news without being overwhelmed by emotion.

The shock response is relatively unemotional—you might be surprised to remember later that you can recall the design on the audiologist's dress or the pattern of shadows on the wall as the doctor broke the news. But one very strong emotion might sweep over you upon learning that your child is really deaf: relief. Consider the parents who have had strong suspicions about their child's ability to hear for over a year before deafness was confirmed. During all this time they struggled to keep hope alive, doing their best to suppress their fears. Every now and then, the intuition that their child was deaf would surface, and they would have to begin again the battle against believing it. This kind of emotional tug-of-war is exhausting. A definitive answer, even if it confirms the parents' worst fears, is bound to be a relief. It is the one way out of the draining cycle of suspicion, fear, and false hope.

Shock is a temporary state, but it is possible to remain in a state of stunned disconnectedness for too long. Some people seem never to get over their shock at the news that their child is deaf and proclaim themselves unable to accept the fact years later. Remaining in shock is an unconscious attempt to hold off comprehension and the strong, painful feelings that accompany it. For example, in one family, the mother, Nancy, was in danger of remaining lost in shock upon learning that her three-year-old son had been left deaf by meningitis. When the doctor gave her the news, she left the boy in the hospital, with her husband coping as best he could. She took a plane to her parents' city and remained at their home for more than six weeks, unable to push past the inertia that overtook her whenever she thought of her boy's deafness. For the entire period, she felt none of the painful emotions that are an inevitable part of the adjustment process.

Nancy had been raised in a wealthy family that value the medical establishment highly. Her parents could afford to consult specialists for any medical problem. She grew up believing that every problem had a cure. When told that her boy was deaf *for life* and that no one could restore his hearing, Nancy was flabbergasted. Not just her son's future but her whole system of beliefs was called into question. She remained stunned for many weeks, but eventually, in the security of her parents' home, she was able to grieve for her own losses and return to her son.

People often realize unconsciously that they need to jar themselves out of shock and allow their feelings to flow freely. Moving like sleepwalkers, they take whatever steps are necessary to force themselves to *feel.* Consider Patricia, who went to a disco the day her mother died. After sitting at her mother's bedside throughout the old woman's illness and finally watching her slip away, Patricia sat with her mother's body for a long while. Then she walked slowly out of the hospital, got into a cab, and asked to be driven to a nightclub. There she danced and danced for six hours straight. Her husband was aghast when she told him where she had been, but Patricia had somehow known that she needed violent and exhausting physical exercise to break down her resistance to the experience of her loss.

A young academic, Edward, shocked his family and friends on the night his daughter was born. When he discovered that the infant, Melissa, had been born without a left arm, he too walked out of the hospital but headed straight for a liquor store. Edward rarely drank, even at parties, but on this night he bought a bottle of bourbon and drank it all down. He got dead drunk: he wept, pounded the walls, bellowed his anger, and finally passed out, leaving his wife to cope with her own feelings alone. In the morning, though suffering from a hangover, he was able to confront the situation clearly and begin to do the things that had to be done. Most importantly, he was able to show his concern and support for his wife, who was having great difficulty accepting the fact of her new baby's handicap. Two years later, the family discovered that Melissa was deaf. For the second time in his life, Edward bought a bottle of bourbon and drank it straight down. By morning he was well out of shock and deep into the second phase of the response cycle, recognition.

Recognition

Following the shock period—the calm before the storm—comes a time of deep and painful emotion. Now the words of the doctor or audiologist have really sunk in and the meaning of what you have been told starts to become clear. Your child is deaf. There is no cure. He or she cannot hear and will never be able to hear.

At this point, you begin to grapple over and over with the same set of facts in the effort to realize fully how your life has changed. Deafness will be a part of your child's—and your own—life forever. It will always have a profound influence on the way your child thinks, feels, and interacts with other people. Above all, deafness will always affect the way your child communicates.

Along with a recognition of what your child's deafness means comes a flood of practical considerations. With four words, "Your child is deaf," your family life has been altered forever. Your plans, your dreams, your budget, and your financial security have all been called sharply into question.

Most of us have some sense of what we can realistically expect out of life. As long as nothing unforeseen happens to challenge those expectations, we take our plans for ourselves and our children pretty much for granted. But the news of a child's deafness can have a shattering effect on our sense of the future. Will our life-styles change? Will our child be normal, like us, or is he or she fated to become a ward of the community, drearily and grudgingly subsidized from cradle to grave? Must we abandon hope for any kind of productive future for the child? And what of the rest of the family? Do we dare have another child, as we planned? Such questions are bound to crowd into your consciousness—prematurely, perhaps, but insistently. Do not attempt to suppress these worries. The questions are natural, as is the anxiety they evoke. Later, when you have grown accustomed to the new circumstances of your family life, you will be able to face these issues more calmly.

Financial worries are natural, too. The doctors, consultants, therapists, hearing aids, special schools—"How will we afford them?" you ask yourself in panic. Many parents are appalled at themselves for thinking of money matters at such a time, but these are real considerations that pose lasting problems. Thinking about them is natural and understandable. In fact, an increasing number of options are available for families of disabled children seeking financial aid. For now, however, the point is not to solve all your financial worries at once but to allow yourself to think about money matters without feeling guilty. You have time to work out solutions. Be reassured that outside help is available and then give yourself the freedom to think about anything that occurs to you. The end product of this surfacing of concerns will be a fuller understanding of your family's real situation.

At this time, too, parents commonly feel overwhelmed by the world they find themselves entering. Deafness is a multifaceted problem: it has a medical aspect, a speech aspect, a social aspect, and an educational aspect. Thus, you might find your doctor or audiologist talking to you about hearing specialists, speech specialists, hearing aid salespeople, family therapists, group therapists, psychological counselors, special clinics, special schools, sign language classes, correspondence courses—the list goes on and on. If you are unused to dealing with professionals and with institutions that require forms, deposits, decisions, and commitments, you are likely to feel frightened or panic-stricken.

One common reaction to being swamped by professionals is withdrawal. To guard yourself against withdrawing, do not force yourself to attend to the vast assortment of professionals right away. Be patient. There will be time to learn about the services available later. Now your need is to adjust to the altered circumstances of your life.

Ideally, you should have someone to protect you at this stage from the onrush of new information, the new vocabulary, and the long list of professional services concerned with the deaf. However, it rarely happens that outsiders can empathize with your confusion or with the enormity of the change in your family life. If both a father and a mother are involved, you can help each other with reminders to be patient and to take the time needed to focus on yourselves. But if you are a single parent coming to terms with your child's deafness alone, try to remember that you will have time later on to become informed and make decisions. Go slowly, one step at a time.

Even more overwhelming than practical considerations at this stage will be your emotional reactions to the knowledge that your child is deaf. Once the initial shock abates you will be swept by feelings, and almost all the feelings will be painful. It is important for you to realize that the feelings that surface are *simply feelings*. Feelings are neither good nor bad; they simply are. A danger lies not in the likelihood that you will experience painful emotions but in the possibility that you will suppress feelings that ought to come out. What follows is a survey of some of the most common feelings that surface in parents when they learn their children are deaf. Take heart from the fact that for everyone these feelings are often intense and self-centered.

Grief

The grief parents feel on learning that their child is deaf is very like the grief one feels at the loss of a loved one. In a sense, the child the parents thought they had has died, to be replaced by another made strange by deafness. On discovering the deafness, the parents must say good-bye forever to the child who was to play out their hopes and dreams. They mourn the child, deeply disturbed at the thought that the baby they thought they knew so well was really someone else all along, a child whose inner life was totally unlike the one they had been imagining.

It is not uncommon for parents to become stranded in grief. We all know people who mourn for years a lost child, parent, or spouse. In such cases it is the bereaved who suffer, but when a deaf child's parents grieve endlessly for their fantasy child, the living child can be damaged by the parents' sorrow. The story of Timothy exemplifies such a situation. Timothy, today a successful landscape architect, somehow managed to mature and develop despite his parents' unabated sadness. They do not think of their son as a success but only as a deaf person. And they view his deafness as an ongoing tragedy despite all Timothy's gains. Everything that goes wrong for Timothy—things that might go wrong for anyone, since no one's life goes according to plan—reawakens his parents' grief, which by now is clearly self-pity. These people seem sorrowful by nature. Their misery drags them down and inhibits them from taking pleasure in Timothy's development and accomplishments. It is almost miraculous that Timothy has found the motivation to succeed in the face of his parents' unhappiness.

Healthy parents who mourn the lost child of their fantasies eventually let the image go, lay it to rest, and turn their attention to the real, living child before them. Soon they find that, yes, the child is different from their original idea of him or her—but only in the inability to hear. The personality of the child that has been unfolding from birth is the same, the identity the child has been forging over the months, the same. Once their grief has passed, parents find that the child they thought they had lost is the child that stands before them.

Guilt, Blame, and Shame

Who does not ask, "Why me?" when something bad befalls them? And who cannot come up with a score of reasons in answer to that question? Parents often indulge in a process of placing blame following the discovery of their child's deafness, very often winding up by taking the blame themselves. "I didn't think we could afford this child. I should have been happier during the pregnancy," a mother might think. "I should have taken better care of my wife during pregnancy, gotten her to eat better," a father might say to himself. Or, "I was a bad girl when I was young. Now I've been punished." Or, "I was so wild as a teenager. No wonder this is happening to me now."

No matter how farfetched, we can always find a crime to fit an imagined punishment. And sometimes the circumstances seem to point unmistakably to a parent's guilt. For example, parents often punish their children for failing to respond to verbal cues *before* they discover the children's deafness. In such circumstances parents have a built-in excuse to feel guilty and to assume responsibility for the impairment. Committing so human an error does not make the parents guilty. Still, it is easy for them to *feel* guilty. And the emotional turmoil often deepens, since guilt breeds shame. For if a parent believes that a child's deafness is a punishment for the parent's misbehavior, it is easy for that parent to believe that the whole world is perceiving it as such: "Everyone will know I called this down on myself. They may not know what I did, but they'll know I got my just deserts."

Feelings of guilt and shame can lead parents to conceal from others for as long as possible the fact that their child is deaf. It is not hard to keep this secret until the child reaches school age. But concealing the fact for too long can delay action necessary to help the child. It is important for your child, then, that you realize when you are using his or her deafness as a symbol of your own guilt. Simply recognizing such a pattern in yourself can be the first step toward breaking it.

Anger

Another source of guilt in parents is the anger and resentment they feel toward the child for being deaf. Let us reiterate the fact that feelings are neither good nor bad; they just are.

Now realize that when your expectations for a happy life are smashed, feelings of anger are inevitable. And since anger seeks a target as surely as water flows downhill, some of the anger you feel will be focused on the agent of change: the child.

It is natural not only to feel such resentment but also to feel horror at feeling it. "But this child is helpless and in need of my care," you will think, almost before you allow yourself to know your feelings. Parents rarely sustain a sense of anger toward their deaf child. Most often they turn their rage onto the professional closest to them or onto themselves. In the latter case, the anger becomes depression, which itself can be a debilitating emotion if unacknowledged and unexpiated.

Ellen, mother of Melissa, the child born deaf and with only one arm, suffered the deadening effects of unexpressed anger. Ellen was a nurse who understood from the beginning what her doubly handicapped child was up against physically. This mother spent much of her energy suppressing her feelings of rage. For months after Melissa's deafness was confirmed, Ellen went through each day woodenly. She felt nothing but a sinking certainty that life would never change, that for her and for Melissa life had leveled out forever on a plane of unhappiness. Fortunately, Ellen met a teacher of deaf children who was able to recognize the extent of Ellen's depression. The teacher invited Ellen into her office and said simply, "I can see that you are in despair." That direct statement penetrated the armor Ellen had assumed to shield herself from her own feelings. Once her defenses were cracked, Ellen's feelings flooded up to overwhelm her. She had a long, cleansing cry followed by an intense conversation with the teacher about Melissa and about Ellen's feelings regarding Melissa's deafness. In that hour, Ellen shook off her months-long depression and began to feel that life was moving on.

Frustration
One emotion parents feel again and again is frustration at their own impotence. Their child is in need and they can do

nothing. The anger they feel at this knowledge often goes unacknowledged and unexpressed. Instead, their thoughts about the child's need often take the form of empathy, a healthy and natural imagining of what deafness feels like. In the effort to identify and empathize, however, some parents go too far, into a reaction called "overidentification." They view the child's deafness as a sudden loss—what they would feel if they suddenly found themselves to be deaf. This imagined condition is very different from what a deaf child really experiences, which, at least until age three or four, is a total acceptance of deafness as the way things are. Such an error in identification, if it continues, can lead parents to mistake a child's needs later on. For instance, in the case of a child's angry tantrum, an overidentifying parent might ascribe the outburst to deafness, whereas the child might actually be expressing fury at the inability to get a point across. In such a case, the parent intent on catching the child's meaning would be doing more good than the parent attempting to empathize with the child's feelings.

An overidentifying parent can also make the mistake of overemphasizing the social isolation deafness can cause. True, deafness does isolate children if parents do not take active steps to provide a social environment in which the child can participate fully. But as ever, the golden mean prevails here. Consider Eric, age fifteen. Eric's mother overidentified with his deafness from the start and was never able to step far enough back to see that other factors—the social and developmental factors that affect everyone, deaf or not—were having strong effects on Eric. She continually focused on the pain he *must* have been feeling (according to her) and was thus always finding problems to tackle on his behalf. For a long time she merely tried to convince the parents in her neighborhood to encourage their children to play with Eric so he would not feel left out. Meddling with Eric's outside social environment to that extent was bad enough, but soon she got the idea of paying two boys to spend time with Eric once a week. In doing so, she set up an artificial environment in which Eric, far from being the beneficiary, was the inevitable victim. It was only a matter of time until Eric learned, much to his humiliation, that his two best friends were really his paid companions. True, Eric's mother was only looking out for his welfare. But if she could have seen that there was more to Eric than his deafness, she would have been closer to accepting him fully and to enhancing his feelings of security.

The tendency to overidentify with the child, especially in the early stages of responding to the new situation, is natural and understandable. Still, as Eric's story demonstrates, it is possible to get stuck at this stage. Again, the solution is to become aware of what you are feeling. Recognizing and acknowledging your feelings will help you to guard against the possibility of acting for the wrong reasons—that is, solely for yourself rather than for the good of your child.

Suppression: A Warning

The recognition phase of the response cycle is a tumultuous time. Throughout this period you will be faced with the dilemma of experiencing fully your own reactions while still being attentive and responsive to your child. In this context, suppressing the painful emotions you experience—anger, frustration, resentment, guilt—is doubly dangerous. Though you are only newly aware of your child's deafness, he or she has been living with and within it from birth. By the age of one or two your child will be astute at reading your facial expressions. A deaf child examining his or her parents' faces is likely to spot clues to suppressed emotion. This acuity might make it hard for you at first to know how to relate to the child through your own unhappiness. But perhaps in becoming aware of your child's ability to read expressions you will feel the first glimmer of hope. After all, reading facial expressions is a very subtle sort of communication, one to be seized upon and developed.

The second danger of suppression, no less important than the first, is the damge you can do yourself by refusing to allow free expression to your responses. The story of Ellen, Melissa's mother, suggests that suppression of emotion can result in depression and despair. Terry, an ex-colleague of Paul Ogden's, serves as another example of the effects of suppression. Terry was a popular instructor at a school where Paul taught and was particularly sympathetic to the deaf students in his classes. One day he discovered that his three-year-old son, Ted, who had just recovered from meningitis, had lost his hearing completely as a result of the disease.*

Terry came to Paul's office to talk about his son, and as they talked Paul became confused, for Terry rambled on and on about the importance of education, even though he had only learned of Ted's deafness that day and was not yet ready to make important decisions. After two hours, he was still talking about how important it was for Ted to get a good education. Paul listened sympathetically, all the while wondering what Terry was feeling inside.

Later, Paul's boss told him that he had talked with Terry and that Terry had cried and expressed grief to him. With Paul, Terry had held back, considerately (because of Paul's deafness) trying not to show how completely tragic he felt deafness to be. With Paul's boss, though, he wept, first because he was afraid his son would grow up to resemble the deaf kids in his class, none of whom could read past first-grade level. He also cried because his wife had left him—she was the woman described earlier, who fled to her parents' home on learning of her son's deafness. Clearly, Terry had a lot to contend with. However, the tears he cried that day were apparently the last he allowed himself to shed. From then on he turned his life into a frenzy of activity—he began shopping around for a hearing aid, making the first inquiries about the best schools in the country, and restructuring his work schedule so he could spend more time with his son.

---

*Ninety percent of those who contract meningitis experience hearing loss and in most cases the loss is about 95 percent of total hearing.

Two months after he first learned of Ted's deafness, Terry showed up with Ted and his mother (she had finally returned after six weeks' absence). The son had lost his balance along with his hearing, but he was gaining it back through activities planned and pursued by his father: swimming, rock climbing, running. Terry reported that the boy had actually become more active since he lost his hearing, not an unusual development, since deaf children often need to be more active than hearing children simply to get feedback from the world.

Four months after discovery, Ted was enrolled in one of the best schools for the deaf in the country. Paul thought it was wonderful that Ted's parents had enrolled him so quickly. But Terry worked in California, and Ted and his mother lived in St. Louis, where the school was located. Terry commuted back and forth for holidays, and the situation was very stressful for him. After a year he called Paul to say he was missing his wife and child deeply and wanted them to come home but was worried about doing the right thing. The head of the school had not given him much comfort. "If you're concerned about your boy," she said, "leave him in school. If you're concerned about yourself, bring him home."

Terry was now clearly suffering on his own behalf. He had been busy every minute since Ted's deafness was confirmed: getting things done, finding things out, organizing, arranging. But he had never taken the time to mourn the hearing boy he had planned for and lived with for the first three years of Ted's life. Now he was weighed down by his own unhappiness and burdened by the guilt his feelings inspired. He finally decided to do something for himself—he brought his family home and enrolled Terry in a less prestigious but satisfactory day school.

The moral of Terry's story is, Take time for yourself. And be *patient.* You need not do everything at once, or make all your decisions today. And you need not give up your sense of life's continuity. With respect to your deaf child, take one day at a time. Try not to view life solely in terms of progress. Above all, respect your own feelings and be aware of them always. No matter how much you want them to, your feelings will not go away.

Denial

The recognition period is a stormy and painful one, and at some point the mind seeks relief from the new knowledge it has been struggling to accept. Thus, almost everyone faced with a painful life change steps back from it at some point, denies its reality, and tries to view the world as it was before. A tendency to deny the reality of your child's deafness is a natural part of your struggle to come to terms with it. It serves as a sort of breathing space to give you rest from the high level of anxiety you have been feeling.

The danger of denial lies not in experiencing it but, again, in becoming fixated on it, failing to move past it to a final acceptance of your child's deafness and constructive action. And again the way to guard against this kind of paralysis is to learn to recognize the denial stage and your own inability to pass through it. Recognition alone will lead you to perceive your situation in a new way and thus to move on toward understanding and action.

Denial takes many forms. Most recognizable is the outright refusal to accept inescapable facts. Denying reality is amazingly easy, especially if you remove yourself from those who might try to convince you of the truth. Therefore, it is common for parents acting out of denial to turn away from the doctors and therapists they have relied on and to seek a miracle cure among people more likely to support their wishful thinking. In this era, with a hundred forms of healing advertised in the back pages of every magazine, it is not hard to find a path that will lead you away from accepting your child's deafness. If you do step off on such a path, maintain a healthy skepticism and do not close off your option to turn back. Remember, the longer it takes you to accept the fact that the deafness is permanent, the longer your child will have to wait for your help.

The story of Pete and his family shows that denial can last a lifetime. Pete is thirty now, and his parents have wanted him to be *normal*—that is, hearing—since they learned that he was deaf, when he was two. He was never allowed to gesture or sign or do anything that might indicate he had a hearing problem. Like many parents unable to accept the facts, Pete's mother and father seemed to think that if Pete *appeared* to hear he would no longer be deaf.

In late adolescence, Pete decided to learn some signs. At first his parents refused their permission, but they finally submitted to his fierce demands, rationalizing his desire by saying that Pete needed signs to become a leader in the deaf community. In fact, Pete is a terrible leader. He had no intention of becoming a standard-bearer for the deaf community. He simply wanted to join it, for companionship.

Still, this one sojourn into the deaf community was not characteristic of Pete. For the most part, he accepted his parents' line—be "normal," look "normal." "Normal" was Pete's favorite word. Recently, he came to Paul after breaking up with what seemed to be his hundredth girl friend—all of whom could hear. He had always flatly refused to date deaf girls, insisting that he had to have a "normal" girl friend. Paul suggested that the instability of his relationships with women might be related to the deaf-hearing combination. Such a combination does not necessarily pose difficulties, but in Pete's case the theory seemed worth considering. Pete exploded at Paul's suggestion. "I want a hearing girl," he stated angrily, "and my mother wants one, too!"

Paul had been giving Pete the benefit of the doubt all during their friendship of many years, but at this remark he finally decided Pete was a hopeless case. Nevertheless, Pete's vain attempts to deny a significant part of himself—his deafness—could not really be blamed on Pete. His parents had been denying his deafness for thirty years. They made all their choices and decisions on the basis of appearances, not in terms of what might be best for Pete, and Pete grew up doing the same thing.

Worse, they made their acceptance—and maybe even their love—of their son contingent on his ability to resemble a hearing person. In denying Pete's deafness, they denied a large part of their son. Now neither his parents nor Pete himself can accept Pete as he is. Little wonder that he has difficulty with his love life.

Denial is sometimes expressed as a neurotically single-minded effort on the part of the parents to teach a deaf child to speak.* In the manner of Pete's parents, such families may even forgo the use of hearing aids** and prohibit the child from using gestures and facial expressions. Again, the mistaken premise here is that a person who speaks is not really deaf—a belief entirely rooted in appearance rather than reality.

Denial sometimes takes the form of frantic activity on behalf of the deaf child or total commitment to programs for the deaf. Parents denying the seriousness of their child's hearing loss direct all their energies to improving the services at the child's school, leaving none for the child at home. We have all heard of the psychiatrist with neurotic children or the family therapist with a rocky marriage. The tendency to obscure the reality of our personal lives by exhausting our energies in more public activities is a common one, and it is not difficult to recognize if you look for it. Think about the way you use your time. Is the energy you are devoting to improving conditions for deaf children in your community sapping energy you might be giving to your child? Are you too tired at the end of the day to give your child the attention and support he or she needs and expects from you?

Denial is natural and inevitable. But the truth is that your

---

*This effort is different from a determined commitment to oralism, discussed in Chapter 4.

**Not all deaf people use hearing aids, but deaf children are encouraged to wear them in case they have residual hearing that can be amplified by the aids. Hearing aids do not guarantee improvement.

child is deaf. Further, ways of helping your child live with deafness do exist. Once you accept this information and find a course of action you can pursue wholeheartedly, denial will give way to acceptance.

Acceptance

Up again goes the emotional seesaw. Suddenly some fact, some observation, some overheard remark, slips into your consciousness from the outside, and you realize fully not only that your child is deaf but that both you and the child can live with the deafness. In the same moment you might realize that your child is separate from you, that you have been undergoing an extreme emotional adjustment while he or she has lived with the deafness all along. Slowly you are able to come out of hiding. You begin to realize that you cannot conceal forever the fact that your child is deaf.

Many parents seem to symbolize their acceptance of their child's deafness by stating the fact publicly. They might begin to inform grandparents and other family members from whom they have guarded their secret before. In telling family and friends, these parents not only identify their child as a deaf child but also tentatively try out a new public role for themselves as well, that of a parent of a child with a hearing impairment. Some self-consciousness is always involved in assuming a new social role. Putting on this particular hat in public takes courage, since it is bound to evoke concern, and perhaps even horror, from others. You are well warned not to spend a lot of energy comforting others who react with sadness to your news. Once you have accepted your child's deafness and begin to take action, your work will be cut out for you. People who turn to you for comfort will be asking more than you can be expected to give.

One educator of deaf children identifies parents in the acceptance stage by the state of their children's hearing aids. He notes that children of parents in the denial stage generally wear their aids under their clothes, have many repair and earmold problems, and often go to school without their aids for one reason or another. When the parents reach acceptance, hearing-aid problems miraculously disappear, the aids are worn freely outside the clothes, and attention is focused on other things. Both parents and children seem able to accept the aids for what they are—limited but useful sound amplifiers—rather than treat them as awkward badges identifying the child as "handicapped."

One clear advantage of discussing your child's deafness publicly is that you can seek out other families with similar problems, simply for the purpose of comparing notes. For example, Lorraine, a divorced mother of three, might have benefited greatly from meeting a mother of a deaf child. Lorraine's children were five years, two years, and eight months of age. The family lived on welfare plus small monthly child-support payments. Their total income put them at what the government deemed subsistence level.

Karen, Lorraine's two-year-old daughter, was diagnosed as profoundly deaf. Lorraine had a very shaky understanding of deafness, as do many people who have never known a deaf person. Basically, she believed deafness to be a speech problem, not a hearing problem. Thus, her struggle to come to grips with her daughter's deafness included coming to grips with the true meaning of deafness.

At the time she learned of Karen's deafness, life was not easy for Lorraine. Her older child, Roberta, was starting school and having trouble adapting, and her younger child was being weaned. The family had no car and depended on public transportation. Karen was being scheduled for appointments with various kinds of therapists and doctors all over the county. Lorraine had to make special appointments with a counselor to get approval for financial-aid payments. Each therapist, doctor, and hearing-aid salesman she met overloaded her with information she could not absorb. Lorraine began to miss appointments and forget the meaning of the new words she was learning. She was in danger of withdrawing from the problem altogether, leaving Karen to get along as best she could.

Lorraine needed exposure to families of deaf children—not just to professionals concerned with deafness. She needed to learn the realities of deafness through *experience*. What she needed above all—and what could only be conveyed to her first-hand, not third-hand through a therapist or a doctor— was proof that it is possible for deaf children to learn, to com- municate, and to lead full rich lives.

Once parents accept their situation, their chief need is to ex- press and understand their feelings. This is another good rea- son to seek out people in similar circumstances. Be warned, however. When you do meet other families of deaf children, do not expect too much, and above all do not *compare* too much. You will be supersensitive to the differences between your child and others you meet. You might be frightened and dis- couraged at the extent of a particular child's communication difficulties. You might be elated and overly encouraged at the progress of another. Remember that each child, each family, each situation, is unique. This is true for everyone, not just deaf children and their families. At the same time, however, get all you can from the parents of the deaf children you meet. Find out how they live. Watch them communicate with their children. Ask them how they got over specific difficulties.

Two families Paul knows are living proof of the benefits of sharing experience. Both families have deaf daughters, now in their teens. The mothers and fathers met through a deaf pro- gram and became friends. The girls are close friends, too. These families exchange information and have come to benefit particularly from their habit of testing on each other informa- tion gathered from outside, and especially from professional sources. They have found that their experience at working through problems day by day has served them better than the advice of the professionals, who are far removed from their family lives. They do not have to take everything told to them as gospel, and they can indulge in skepticism without fearing that they might disregard important information. These parents and their daughters are healthy and balanced.

DEALING WITH PROFESSIONALS: A SIDENOTE

The anecdote above demonstrates another important principle: Maintaining a healthy skepticism with respect to professionals is both valuable and necessary. With each other's support, these families have been able to shed the worshipful attitude that most of us have been trained to take toward the medical profession. They have learned that the experts can be wrong.

Still, professionals trained in the field of deafness can provide you with precisely the information and support you need. The problem lies in learning how to take what you need without becoming confused. Eventually, with experience, you will learn to deal with the experts. At the beginning of your association the best advice you can have is, Ask questions. Professionals can be brusque, insensitive, and intimidating—as anyone can. You might feel yourself at a disadvantage, and indeed you are, for you are struggling to adapt to circumstances you may barely comprehend. You might feel nervous about demanding a full and clear explanation. But remember, the doctors and therapists are there *to serve your needs.*

To sort out those professionals whose expertise you can trust, learn to challenge the experts if what they say isn't clear. Ask them to explain their points more fully or to explain again in words you understand. Those who really know what they are doing, and who know that their true role is to serve you, will work with you until you have understood fully. Those who disappear or who add to your confusion are not worth pursuing—look for someone else.

Recognizing a responsible professional takes time and experience. Still, a few tips can help. First, try to determine whether a doctor or therapist *really knows* deaf people and parents of deaf children. Lots of people have book learning, but practical experience is what counts. Also, be aware that often the best ear doctors know nothing about the experience of deafness, the psychology of deafness, deaf communities, and so on. Ask your doctor for referrals but do not rely on him or her for this kind of information. Finally, beware of "name droppers"— people who claim that they have lots of deaf friends and therefore can advise you on the best route to take. No one knows all the answers for you and your family. You will have to make the final decisions based on information you gather yourself. Ask those name droppers for introductions to their deaf friends—not for advice.

CONSTRUCTIVE ACTION

A number of methods of communication and many combinations of methods are open to deaf people. In the course of your child's education, especially in the early years, you will learn of these options. Many a therapist or teacher will try to convince you that his or her way is the only right way, and you will be faced with many decisions that have important consequences for your child. The course you finally settle on will be based solely on your personal choice. The point of encouraging you to respond freely and fully to the knowledge of your child's deafness—besides protecting your own well-being, of course—is to enable you to think clearly in making such choices. You will need stability and perseverance to learn about all the options available for helping your child communicate and for judging which ones are suitable to his or her individual needs.

Methods of communication are explored later in this book. At this point the emphasis is not on methods but on support. You are first and foremost a parent, not a teacher. It is from the security and support you supply as a parent that your child will gain the motivation to develop his or her communication and social skills—two aspects of life that deafness affects most strongly.

Together, the following stories of two families illustrate the importance to a deaf child of total acceptance and support. The first is the family of Melissa, now fifteen, who was born both missing an arm and deaf, a victim of her mother's rubella. Melissa's father, Edward, was the man who got drunk on learning of his daughter's disabilities. Both times Edward's extreme responses were short-lived. Almost overnight he reentered family life and, along with his wife, undertook to do all he could to learn Melissa's special needs and the best ways of serving them. Ellen, Melissa's mother, shook off her depression to provide Melissa with the inner strength to compensate for her disabilities. The family had been close-knit and loving before Melissa was born, and it pulled together even more closely when her disabilities were identified. Melissa was sent to an oral school (oralism is discussed in Chapter 4) and learned to use speech as her primary mode of communication. Further, she became a highly social young lady and in late childhood joined a Little League baseball team as a pitcher, despite her missing arm.

The second family is that of Don, a biologist, now thirty-one. Don's parents chose not to pursue the oral method. Instead, after considerable research into the methods of communication open to deaf people, they turned their attention to helping Don to read and write well. Don had speech lessons, too, but his academic skills developed much more quickly than his speech skills. Don did very well in school using the skills his parents made sure he acquired. He was salutatorian at Gallaudet College in Washington, D.C. (the only liberal arts college for the deaf in the world) and got a Ph.D. in biology at the University of Minnesota. Throughout his life his parents have supported him in everything he did. Today Don has a rich and full life, both professionally and socially.

The common denominator shared by Don and Melissa, despite the fact that they learned different methods of communication, was family support. Both families took an interest in their children as human beings, not just as deaf people, and made sure they acquired means of expressing themselves as individuals. The method each family provided was different, but the end product—a well-adjusted, active, freely communicating individual—was the same. Both families went through all the stages of the response cycle described in this chapter and emerged with new energy for constructive action.

*   *   *

You are poised on the brink of a new education along with your child. The child will learn to communicate and take a place in the world, but you will share in his or her triumphs, disappointments, and renewals. A therapist who counsels families with children who have disabilities quotes in his book* a number of clients and adds some reflective remarks of his own. As a parent just beginning a new learning process with your deaf child, you could do no better than to take heart from these words, spoken by a parent who has gone before you:

> "I now feel that I have a purpose, that my values are so much better since we have had this child. I would have been a bored suburban housewife, entertaining myself by going to coffee klatches and bridge games. I now know what is important and my life has a purpose. I never realized how much joy there is in having this child. Every time he says something I swell up with pride and happiness. Each thing he does is such a milestone and we all delight in it."
>
> I have heard statements like [this] so many times that I no longer pity parents of a hearing-impaired child. I have come to recognize that the child offers a very rare opportunity for the parents to grow, albeit through much pain and travail. For many parents, the raising of a handicapped child has led to a fundamental changing of values and to an enhancement of living. One parent has said, "I would be the last person in the world to tell anyone that [a disability] is a happy circumstance; yet when our child was born, if just one person had come to us to tell us that despite our sadness there was hope, that this was not the end of the world, but rather a challenge and a uniting force that could bring out the very best in each member of the family, how much more bearable our grief would have been."

---

*David Lutermann, *Counseling Parents of Hearing Impaired Children* (Boston: Little, Brown & Co., 1979), pp. 14–15.

Chapter 2

A Healthy Family Environment

ONCE YOU HAVE ADJUSTED to the fact that your child is deaf, you will be anxious to begin making whatever changes are necessary in the way you live. But what are these changes to be? What special needs does a deaf child have that only the family can meet?

In the past it was the fashion among some educators to encourage parents to treat a deaf child as they would a hearing child of the same age. But this approach creates problems, for in fact deaf children do differ significantly from hearing children in the ways they receive and transmit messages. Therefore, a more constructive approach is for parents to provide the deaf child with the same information, guidance, and emotional support they would provide a hearing child of the same age, but to expect to use different *means* in doing so.

If you have raised other, hearing children, you know how much children learn simply by absorbing what they hear. How often have you looked up at your hearing child and asked, "Now, where in the world did she pick *that* up?" Hearing children begin to learn by listening long before they can talk. Often they seem to come equipped with "family knowledge"—

the beliefs, customs, opinions, and understandings held in common by family members—even when parents put little conscious effort into instilling such knowledge.

Deaf children have no access to the casual conversation, dinner-table talk, bedtime question sessions, or other auditory activities in which such family information is exchanged. *Everything deaf children learn must be taught to them.* And though young children learn many social skills and the rudiments of academic skills in nursery and preschools, they learn the most basic facts of life within the family. Therefore, although you are primarily the parent, not the teacher, of your young deaf child, you must learn to view yourself as something of an interpreter. Everything that happens in your household has meaning, but that meaning will be unavailable to your deaf child until you consciously make it available. The child will look to you to explain family relationships, rules of conduct, manners and courtesies, moral standards, and the way things are done. If you do not convey to the child this basic information about the world, who will?

SPECIAL COMMUNICATION NEEDS

The crucial factor in creating a healthy home environment for a deaf child is good communication. To demonstrate the importance of a free flow of communication between parent and child, consider the following situation, in which the communication between a deaf child and his parents is far from satisfactory.

Jimmy, age four, and Charlie, age three, are going on a trip to Grandma's house. Jimmy, a hearing boy, has been anticipating the trip for weeks. He knows that he will go on a big airplane, that he will fly high in the sky, and that when he gets to Grandma's his parents will leave him there while they go off on a trip of their own.

Charlie, who is deaf, begins to perceive that something unusual is going on during the week before the journey. He notices that the family routine has been disrupted and that clothes are being washed and piled around the living room and then stacked in strange brown boxes with handles. He gets the idea, on the day of departure, that the family is going somewhere, but he does not know where, for how long, or why— and no one attempts to clear up the mystery. Both of Charlie's parents believe his deafness to be a barrier to communication of any sort. They stopped trying to reach him shortly after they learned he was deaf.

Jimmy can barely contain his excitement when the family reaches the airport. He presses his nose to the plate-glass windows to watch the big jets arrive. But Charlie does not recognize the huge silver giants as the tiny dots he's seen flying in the sky. He has no idea what they are and is frightened by the tremendous vibrations he feels from their engines. The farthest thing from his mind is that he might enter one. And fly? Even when he is five miles in the sky he fails to understand where he is. All he knows is that the thrum of the engines and the bumpiness of the ride are uncomfortable and that his ears feel peculiar.

When the family finally reaches Grandma's house, Charlie has no idea who this gray-haired woman is. He certainly does not expect his parents to leave him and his brother with this stranger. But after much hugging and kissing, which vaguely reassures Charlie, his mommy and daddy walk out the door.

Charlie is inconsolable. He is frightened of his grandma. He has never met an old person before (except when he was too young to remember), and Grandma's gray hair reminds him of a scary picture of an old, gnarled woman he saw in a book. Furthermore, he has never been left anywhere overnight. He fears that his parents are never coming back, and after three days he is certain of it. He drifts from anger and loneliness into depression. No one can convince him to come away from the door, where he lies by the hour with his cheek on the rug.

In retrospect, Charlie's reactions all make sense. He picked up clues about what was going on around him, but they were false clues. To come to the right conclusions, Charlie would have had to have all the information that had been made available to Jimmy through auditory messages. Regarding the *content* of communication, deaf and hearing children do not differ. The *means* of communication do differ, but the topics parents "discuss" with their deaf children and the thoroughness with which they cover them should be the same.*

In the ideal home setting, the chief job of Charlie's parents regarding the trip would have been to convey the following information to their deaf son: We're going on a wonderful trip to Grandma's house; we're going on a big, loud airplane that flies high in the sky; Grandma is Mommy's mommy and loves you and Jimmy very much; after a while Mommy and Daddy are going away, and you are going to stay with Grandma and have fun and go to the zoo and go to the movies, and so on.

As Charlie's story demonstrates, the chief danger for deaf children is that they will be left out of the communication process altogether, that their need and ability to communicate, even on a nonverbal level, will go unrecognized. You alone can protect your child from becoming isolated. You are the guardian of your child's right to communicate with others. As such, it is your role to create an atmosphere in which communication not only goes on around your deaf child but invites the child's participation as well.

But *how*? you might well ask. How can we get through to each other if my child cannot hear? In the context of deafness, *communication* means the exchange of ideas and information by *any* possible means, not just speech. In the world at large, where speech is the primary method of communication, your child is bound to meet with difficulties and obstacles. Within the home, however, with imagination and freedom from prejudice, you can create an environment in which ideas and infor-

---

*At this point we will pass over the question of *how* one conveys such information to a young deaf child. Simply be reassured that you *can* learn to understand each other. Methods of communication—nonverbal, manual, speechreading, fingerspelling, and oral—are covered in Chapters 3 and 4.

mation flow freely *by whatever means* are necessary to get them across. You will learn to communicate nonverbally, using gestures, facial expressions, and postures. Perhaps you will learn sign language and fingerspelling. In the early years, before formal schooling in a specific method begins, you will be relying most on body language.

Still, in relying on body language you should in no way feel inhibited from speaking and inviting your child to enter the world of speech however he or she is able. Your deaf child needs to learn how speech functions in the hearing world and will do so only if he or she is encouraged to pay attention to it. In short, your child cannot fail to benefit from exposure to *any and all modes of communication.*

The Role of Conversation

Conversation is our principal means of informal communication. This means of interacting involves much more than just the give and take of dialogue. A whole range of social skills and understandings shapes and governs conversation. The sooner your deaf child becomes an active participant in conversations, whatever the communication method he or she uses, the sooner the child will learn these related social skills.

Mothers and fathers should do everything they can to promote exposure and practice in conversation. In the beginning, they must strain to provide and sustain social interaction with the deaf child, even before he or she is able to respond clearly. They can do this by taking both roles in a conversation when the child is unable to respond, by giving the child feedback as to the appropriateness of his or her responses, by letting the child know when his or her reactions are comprehensible and incomprehensible, and even by converting the child's nonverbal responses into explicit verbal ones, in a step toward introducing language.

Children who are encouraged to take part in family conversations in whatever ways they can will begin to take the process for granted rather than feeling shut out by it.

The Importance of Books

Books are another important means of exposing a deaf child to communication. Deaf children in particular can benefit from an early introduction to books and the function of written language. Later in life, many deaf children are able to gain through books much of the information lost to them when younger due to their disability. But deaf children can partake of the world of books only if they are comfortable there and have learned to read well. Thus, early exposure is necessary. Chapter 5 contains specific information on choosing and reading books. For the moment, the important point is that books should play a central role in the life of every deaf child, beginning as soon as the child responds with interest to pictures.

The Time Communication Takes

Deaf children have the same needs as hearing children not only to understand others but also to express themselves. As a parent you will soon realize that few people outside the family have the patience and sensitivity necessary to attend constantly to your child's need to express and receive messages. Thus, your major role will lie in simply being attentive.

One of the realities of deafness is that regardless of the method used, both functions of communication—expressing and receiving information—require a tremendous amount of energy, far more than communicating with a hearing child of the same age. Getting your point across to a deaf child takes at least twice as much time as with hearing children, and capturing a deaf child's message accurately can involve many minutes of guessing and puzzling.

Therefore, listening to a deaf child involves more than just responding to the child's message. It requires that you keep your face to the child at all times, maintain steady eye contact, and focus your concentration completely. Further, it requires that you send test messages back to make sure you have picked up the original message accurately. Conversely, sending messages to your deaf child, as Chapter 3 will explain, requires that you use your whole body, your whole face, and often the most creative area of your imagination.

Maintaining this kind of attentiveness is draining. It is without a doubt the most demanding aspect of raising a deaf child. Yet it is also the most essential for the well-being of your child. With a hearing child you can often communicate important information while doing other things—you can prepare a meal, for example, while discussing traffic safety without having to devote your primary energies to shaping your message. With a deaf child communication *always* takes precedence over *all* other activities. When you and your child are communicating with each other, nothing else can be going on.

SPECIAL SOCIAL NEEDS

We turn now to a range of more general considerations. Although the topics treated in this section are less obviously related to communication, it is important to remember that in every case meeting your child's special social needs depends on the existence of rich and varied communication within the family. As will become clear, unless your child participates in the exchange of ideas and information among family members, your efforts to forge a sense of security and encourage healthy social development will be in vain. In everything you do as a parent of a young deaf child our original dictum applies: The key to a healthy family life is good communication.

We will have occasion in this section to cite a number of examples in which parents remained unaware of their deaf children's special needs. But examples can illustrate successes as well as less happy results. Therefore, we begin with the story of Anastasia, whose parents, Gail and Steven, were unusually sensitive to the needs of a young deaf child.

Anastasia's Story

Gail and Steven have two daughters—Anastasia, who is deaf, and Annemarie, a year younger, who is hearing. At the time Anastasia's deafness was discovered, when she was two and a half years old, both parents had an egalitarian attitude toward child rearing, believing that they could and should spend equal time and give equal attention to each of their children. Over the next few years, however, they came to realize that communicating took more time and energy with Anastasia than with Annemarie. Ultimately, they agreed that the fair thing to do, given Anastasia's deafness, was to give her the extra time and attention she needed. They found ways to compensate for the imbalance with Annemarie when she was young. As the hearing girl grew older, they made sure she fully understood why they gave more time and attention to her sister: not because they loved Anastasia more but simply because she was deaf. During all the years of the girls' childhood and adolescence, Gail and Steven always considered the effects of Anastasia's deafness not only on the hearing-impaired girl but on her hearing sister as well.

Both Gail and Steven have a strong sense of fairness. They realized early that Anastasia's deafness in no way required them to deprive either Annemarie or themselves of their particular needs and pleasures. Both parents were addicted to rock concerts during the mid-sixties, when their daughters were little girls. Early on, they decided that although Anastasia could not hear the music, she could still experience the excitement and visual stimulation at the concerts. Therefore, they made the concerts family events. True to their prediction, Anastasia loved the crowds and the atmosphere on their outings.

Sometimes, however, Anastasia seemed bored and irritable at the concerts, and her parents wondered whether perhaps they were expecting too much in hoping she would enjoy them. But instead of giving up their own fun, Steven hit upon the idea of showing Anastasia how to discriminate among the various vibrations she was feeling from the music and to relate them visually to the individual instruments. First he would act out particular sounds by duplicating their exact rhythm with his hands; then, moving up as close to the musicians as he could, he would show Anastasia which musicians' own hands matched his. Once she caught on, Anastasia loved to stand close to the stage and watch the musicians. From then on she was able to enjoy not only the crowds and atmosphere of the concerts but, visually at least, the music as well.

It was exceptionally sensitive of Steven to realize that Anastasia had been unable on her own to make the connection between the instruments and the vibrations. Many hearing people would have assumed that the connection was obvious. Others, on the other end of the spectrum, would have considered her incapable of discriminating well enough among the various vibrations to associate them with individual instruments. Steven followed his hunch that she did have this capacity. He could have been wrong, but his guess paid off in Anastasia's deeper enjoyment.

Both Gail and Steven have always been firm and consistent in disciplining their daughters. But over the years they have discovered that in some cases they need to think out matters of discipline carefully to make sure that Anastasia's deafness is not influencing the situation in a way requiring special treatment. Many children learn to use their deafness to worm out of unpleasant responsibilities, especially if their parents indulge them. "No, no," they complain. "I can't do math. It's too hard and I don't understand the teacher." In a lenient family such a cry is liable to make math magically disappear. But some things *are* made more difficult by deafness. Parents need to be able to recognize when deafness is influencing a situation before they make a decision regarding discipline.

A good example of this difficulty occurred when Anastasia joined the junior high school swim team. Once she began to compete, she consistently lost races even though she made winning time in practice. She became very depressed and seemed to be losing confidence in herself. At one point she complained that she was losing time at the start of each race because she could not hear the starting gun and had to wait for a visual clue. Because she was so upset, her parents were uncertain whether this was a real problem or whether she was using her disability to excuse her losses. After watching several races they assured themselves that Anastasia did indeed lag behind the others in entering the water, and they arranged for a red flag to be dropped when the starting gun sounded. This was a case of attentiveness to the situation that went beyond the actual exchange of information.

Anastasia was raised to understand that she could and should be independent in spite of her deafness. As soon as she was old enough to go off alone, she was sent by herself to the store or to play in the park. Because they were only a year apart, the sisters were very close. But the parents separated them from time to time, sending each off to a different friend's house or one to a movie and the other to the park. Gail and Steven saw the danger in allowing Anastasia to depend on Annemarie for her hearing. Both girls would have suffered from overdependency—Annemarie in being overburdened by responsibility and Anastasia in losing self-sufficiency. The parents' emphasis on self-reliance and their unswerving confidence in their girls paid off. At this writing, Anastasia is twenty-one and has recently traveled on her own all over Europe. Annemarie will be beginning a similar journey as this book goes to press.

Gail and Steven's chief asset as the parents of a young deaf child was their sensitivity to issues that deafness can raise within a family. They recognized early that Anastasia's deafness alone made her different from Annemarie. But they understood that the difference lay only in Anastasia's powers of communication, not in her inner life as an individual. They knew that they could never ignore their daughter's deafness and always had to consider it in making decisions. But they never saw Anastasia as set apart by deafness. Instead, they did everything necessary to reach her and to enable her to express herself.

Being Explicit

You may have noticed that Gail and Steven were not only very good parents of a deaf child but very good parents in all respects. Analogously, a healthy family environment for a deaf child does not differ in kind from that for a hearing child. It differs only in degree. Whereas both hearing and deaf children need to have the world explained to them, deaf children's parents must make their explanations more explicit, never assuming that the child will "just know." Time and again and under all circumstances, these parents must make absolutely certain that they are not inadvertently leaving their children out by failing to give them the information they need.

Everything that can be assumed or taken for granted in raising a hearing child must be made explicit for a deaf child. Thus, accompanying our first rule—"Good communication is the key to good family life"—is a second, simpler rule: "Be explicit." The sections that follow cover circumstances of family life in which this rule is particularly important.

Making Your Love Explicit

Children are extremely sensitive to their parents' feelings for them, especially in the early stages of life. Often, too, children are much more fragile than adults give them credit for. We have all seen what happens when even the toughest preschooler on the block suddenly senses that his or her parents disapprove of an action. The face crumbles, the eyes fill, and play is forgotten as the child struggles to regain the lost sense of security. Deaf children need the sense of security and affectionate support that any children need, and here perhaps above all the rule to be explicit applies.

Parents affirm a hearing child's sense of accomplishment and security in many ways that a deaf child cannot benefit from. For example, most people, when being told something by another, give little hums of interest or grunts of assent to encourage the speaker to continue. A hearing child telling you of the events of the day at school can take encouragement from these subverbal sounds, but deaf children have no access to auditory clues of their hearers' interest. Therefore, parents must make their interest and approval very clear. Otherwise, even in this seemingly minor way they risk communicating indifference.

Constant parental reassurance and attentiveness are particularly important as deaf children reach age four or five, when they begin to realize that they are different from others. Remember what it feels like to be odd-one-out as a child? And remember how hard children are on the child who is "different"? A child becoming aware that he or she is different might wonder, "If I'm not the same as other children or as my brothers and sisters, perhaps that means I'm not as good. My parents might love me less than they love the others." The thoughtless treatment that many disabled people receive in society only reinforces this feeling. Therefore, deaf children have an intense need to feel wholly accepted and valuable. As parents, you must recognize and respond to this need overtly, with physical and verbal expressions of love and acceptance.

Feeling Love Fully

It's easy to exhort parents to love their children fully, but sometimes *feeling* that love fully is not easy for parents. What happens if a parent *wants* to love and reassure the child but is blocked by feelings of resentment and disappointment at the child's deafness? As we noted in Chapter 1, such feelings are neither uncommon nor unnatural. But children who are well practiced at reading their parents' facial expressions will have no difficulty detecting such negative feelings and will suffer from a suspicion that they are less than fully loved and accepted. How can parents in the grip of such feelings do the best for their children?

Clearly, parents have to sort out such problems for themselves. But a step toward resolving ambivalence is to make sure you are not confusing the child with the deafness itself. The child is not merely a "deaf person." The child is a full human being with an identity and personality distinct from, though of course influenced by, the disability. The deafness is as impersonal as brown hair or blue eyes. Yet many parents think *only* of the deafness when thinking of their deaf child, as if that quality alone defined the individual.

The story of Linda demonstrates the effects of such confusion. Linda's father is a doctor, a well-to-do man with a professional understanding of Linda's deafness. Nevertheless, he has always treated Linda differently from his other children: he spent money on her while giving more freely of his time to the others. Despite his medical knowledge, he clearly viewed her as different—and, from Linda's point of view at least, repellent.

As an adult, Linda likes to receive attention and expects it all the time. But her self-esteem is very low, and she never feels secure in her social relationships. She is like any spoiled child, hearing or deaf. She is short-tempered, inconsiderate, and self-centered, while all the while she feels uncertain of others' true feelings for her. She has always believed her father saw only a deaf person when he looked at her. Whether Linda's father truly confused her with her disability or whether she only believes he did, the effect is the same. The real source of the damage is her father's failure to convey affection for Linda as a person, apart from her deafness.

Withholding Love

A second problem related to feeling love fully is that of withholding love until a condition is met. Recall the story of Pete in Chapter 1, whose parents could only love him if he kept up the pretense of being "normal." They wanted so much for their child to succeed at learning to speak that they unconsciously withheld their love, setting it up as a reward. Many parents who give this impression *do* love their children and do not at all hold back their affection, but by putting great emphasis on succeeding they have the same effect. The message perceived by the child is, "I love you now, but I'll *really* love and accept you *fully* when you learn to talk" (or sign, or whatever is the goal the parents have set up).

Parents who send this message are fighting a losing battle,

since the first prerequisite for success in such a difficult and demanding task as learning to talk is a strong base from which to work: a secure sense of acceptance, security, being well loved, and so on. This is not to say that children who doubt their parents' love for them will not learn to talk or to communicate by some other method. It does imply, however, that such children will face difficult problems, as does anyone who has misgivings about his or her acceptability as a person.

The Household versus the Outside World

Though you can shape your household to meet your child's special needs, your home does not exist in a vacuum. Even if you have the healthiest attitudes toward deafness, the outside world will make itself felt. And the world is not easy on disabled people, even at a time when some old prejudices and misconceptions regarding handicaps are breaking down.

You might feel you can protect your child from the outside world at least until he or she reaches school age. But children begin to thrive on interactions with other children long before they enter school. A deaf child can learn social skills *and* all-important communication skills by relating to other children. Therefore, you are encouraged to make every effort to expose your deaf child early to other children, both hearing and deaf. At the same time, be warned: Your child will be hurt. Among the "hearies," as deaf children refer to the hearing, your child will be the "different" one, the one whom even kind children stare at and single out. Making matters worse will be the inevitable obstacles the child will meet with in a world that seems to have no time to allow a disabled person to learn by trial and error.

In this context, expecting deaf children to take easily to the society of their peers is to make an already difficult situation impossible. A child who is coping with insults and misunderstandings should not have to face parental disappointment as well. Again, the child's primary need from the family is a sense of security, comfort, and the certainty that he or she is fully accepted, whatever the bullies on the block might say.

There is no getting around it: Leaving your protected home and entering the more social, business-as-usual world will not be easy for either you or your child. And yet holding back and living behind closed doors would result in even greater pain for your child in the long run. Introducing your child to that outside world and providing a home to which he or she can return and in which he or she can gain new confidence before venturing out again are important aspects of your responsibility as a parent. A hearing child will learn the ropes in society by imitation and the repetition of auditory cues. But the deaf child will need more explicit guidance from you, and in this capacity you will do best to take each day as it comes, attempting to think of each incident as an experience rather than a test your child must pass or fail.

Fostering Independence
The whole point of giving children a firm base in childhood and working hard to impart social skills to them is not so they can live with you forever, but so they can eventually leave home and operate as individuals with productive futures.

At first, of course, no child ventures out alone. But parents can take a very early first step toward fostering independence outside the home by seeking some form of child care. Every family has different needs and feelings about what age a child is ready to be left with a sitter for the first time. This decision is a personal one influenced by a multitude of factors. But once you reach the decision to place your child in the care of others from time to time, both you and the child will benefit from a consistent schedule of baby-sitting that allows you a break from each other.

Finding a sitter or a play group you trust is the most difficult aspect of establishing a child-care routine. You do not need a professional deaf educator for the job; you need someone with whom your child intuitively feels rapport. But once you find the person or people you trust, these breaks will serve a twofold purpose. Not only will you benefit in terms of rest and renewal, but your child will realize early that he or she can function without you. Scheduled, predictable, safe separation thus becomes the first step toward independence, and its importance cannot be overemphasized. You would do well to view it as one of the essentials of your child's life.

In some circumstances, where family tensions run high, getting off on your own may be literally the only feasible solution. One family Paul knows was nearly shattered by the irritation and repressed anger each member harbored against the others. The parents had two boys—one hearing, one deaf—and, unlike Gail and Steven, were particularly insensitive to what was happening to themselves and to their sons. The oldest boy, Ron, a hearing child, was continually hurt and angered by the fact that his parents never had time to watch him play baseball. The deaf child, Toby, was basically unaware of what was going on around him, for instead of attempting to find ways of communicating with him his parents ran themselves ragged taking him from hearing specialist to psychologist, to clinic, to doctor. Thus Toby suffered constant frustration at his inability to understand what was going on or to express himself to others. The one firm rule in the family, apparently motivated by a misconceived sense of responsibility, was that Toby, although four years old, was never to be left with a sitter. Thus, when Paul met the family it had been literally four years since the parents had been out together for an evening. Their own relationship had the lowest priority in the family as far as demands on their attention was concerned. As a result, their marriage was a sad mixture of mutual misunderstandings, resentments, and exhaustion. What they needed above all was a vacation away from the boys, but the mother would not hear of it. The parents balanced on the brink of divorce until Toby went to day school at age four and a half. When his mother could not deny the fact that he did very well without her at school, she consented to start looking into child care and to begin arranging a holiday with her husband.

Physical separation is only one aspect of the process of instilling a sense of independence in a child. As we saw in Anastasia's case, parents' attitudes toward independence are expressed in the amount of confidence they have in their children. Thus, a parent cannot hope to raise independent children without believing sincerely in the value of self-reliance. Part of the difficulty for many parents is that raising independent children, especially children with disabilities, is a matter not of encouraging but of *allowing* the child to rely on himself or herself.

At first, it is difficult to see how a deaf child can be independent at all. In the early years, the child relies on parents for everything. But the key to enabling yourself to let go is to separate the notions of closeness and dependence. You can be intimate and helpful without engendering utter dependence. You can be loving without being overprotective. You can allow your child to do things, and instruct him or her on how to do them, without actually doing them yourself. As the child grows older, you will be expressing your love by allowing him or her the opportunity to make mistakes. Without this chance, learning cannot occur.

The story of Robert demonstrates that even parents who value independence can cheat their deaf children of the right to make their own mistakes. Both Robert's parents, Rose and Michael, are full-time workers. They live on a ranch and have always placed a lot of importance on raising their three children to think for themselves. By the age of six, Robert, deaf from birth, decided he wanted to be a veterinarian.

In keeping with their rugged ranch life, the parents gave each of their three children ten head of cattle and a horse, and by age eleven each child was expected to take over full responsibility in caring for the animals. But as Robert grew up he began to notice that his parents were not as strict with him as with the other children. They punished his siblings more harshly and constantly found excuses for poor, deaf Robert. "Oh, Robert couldn't hear the alarm clock. That's why he didn't feed the animals this morning"; or "Oh, let Robert enjoy what he's doing. His pleasures are so limited. I'll exercise his horse." Strangely, the older Robert grew, the more frequently his parents excused his lapses, blaming them on his deafness.

When Robert was sixteen, his parents let him take the car whenever he liked, though they strictly limited his brother and sister's use of the car. Rose and Michael felt that Robert needed the car more, since he was incapable of enjoying music or conversation as easily as the others. The worst part was that they carried their laxness over into Robert's academic life. Robert's sister and brother were both given deadlines for finishing college; their parents warned them that they would not pay for college past four years. Both got through on time and did well. But Robert, under no such deadline, dawdled his way through college and took seven years to complete his undergraduate work. He grew up to have almost no self-discipline, and he never did fulfill his childhood ambition to be a vet. Now, as an adult, he resents the deferential treatment he received, especially since he believes it resulted in a self-indulgent streak in his personality. He has a steady job and makes a fair living for himself, but he knows that with work he could have achieved more.

Clearly, Michael and Rose should have applied the standards of self-sufficiency and responsibility equally to all three siblings, deaf or not. At the same time, in Robert's case they would have had to be much more attentive and more explicit in their expectations than with their hearing children. Instead, by allowing Robert special privileges because of his deafness, they protected him from failure in the short run but deprived him of the chance to succeed in any larger sense. Something in their laxness said, "Look, Robert, you might as well not aspire to be self-sufficient; you'll never make it anyway. Let us give you a hand." Deaf children have the potential to live rich, varied, and full lives pursuing the goals they choose. Overindulgent and overprotective parents have the power to quash that potential and instill in their deaf children dependency and defeat.

Discipline

Though our activities seem self-directed as we go through our daily lives, to a large extent life in society, like life inside the home, is governed by rules and mutual understandings. We cross the street when the light is green; we wait when the light is red. We go to school or work on time each morning and get reprimanded if we are late. We pay for our food before leaving a restaurant, we stand in line to get into a movie, we listen politely when someone speaks to us, and we don't interrupt.

Parents convey such rules of behavior to their children, mostly by example. Even before they are nursery-school age, most hearing children have picked up the rudiments of social behavior and simple courtesy if their families practice them. The responsibility of parents to teach social behavior is another of those issues that are taken for granted in the raising of a hearing child but that parents of deaf children must think about consciously. Remember: *Everything deaf children learn they have to be taught.* All the patterns that hearing people take for granted and that hearing children learn by imitation must be identified and explained painstakingly to a deaf child.

The key word in conveying standards of behavior to a deaf child is *clarity*. First you must make sure the rules you set up are clearly understood—"Never blow your nose on your clothes"; "Don't throw balls in the house"; "Don't eat with your hands." Next you must make sure the child understands *why* the rules exist—"Because it ruins your clothes and disgusts other people"; "Because you might break something"; "Because you'll get all dirty and look awful."

As an adult, you might think that the logic behind your *no* is clear and that your reasons for saying it are self-evident, but this is not necessarily so. Where you think you are enforcing a set of rules that make sense, the child might be experiencing a long series of *no*'s that have no relationship to one another. Again, in raising a deaf child you cannot afford to assume that he or she has made the logical connection that seems obvious to you. One boy, for instance, was taught to say "Excuse me" every time he belched. He followed the rule flawlessly at home, where he lived alone with his mother, but in his class at school, applying the rule as he knew it, he said "Excuse me" in turn to every student in the class until he was stopped. His mother had not used her imagination in considering how the boy would generalize the rule outside the home.

Once the rules are clear, the next issue is punishment. Though different parents hold different philosophies on the subject, all seem to agree that some form of punishment is in order when children break or disregard the standards they have established. Again, *clarity* is the key word in punishing deaf children, for unless you make the reason for the punishment very clear the child might fail to connect it with the crime. Punish as soon as the child misbehaves. That old tried-and-true threat "Just wait until your father comes home" is particularly inappropriate with a young deaf child (its merits are questionable for a hearing child as well, for more subtle reasons). He or she might well miss the point of delayed punishment altogether, feeling unjustly treated and puzzled rather than properly chastised for misbehaving.

Teaching Right and Wrong

The subject of discipline leads naturally into a broader area: that of right and wrong. Be aware that you are solely responsible for your child's moral education, at least until he or she enters school. Once again, this simple-sounding rule applies to the hearing child as well, but the deaf child needs explicit instruction in matters that hearing children might pick up without conscious direction.

Consider the area of social behavior and manners. Courtesy is not instinctive; manners and considerate behavior have to be learned. Though most hearing children pick up acceptable behavior through imitation and from auditory cues, deaf children have to be told and shown how to act. The responsibility is on you to save your child—and yourself, for that matter—from instances of social embarrassment.

The responsibility for teaching right and wrong goes a lot further than simple courtesy, however. To a great extent, moral values in general are learned within the family, whether or not the children interpret their parents' beliefs accurately. The story of Miriam demonstrates the importance of fully explaining the abstract concepts that relate to daily life.

Miriam, deaf from birth, was raised in a strict Catholic family that followed the Catholic code of values to the letter. Miriam's mother imposed the faith on Miriam from birth but never explained anything about Catholicism, the rituals involved, or the relation between the religion and the way the family lived. Miriam went to church every Sunday and on holidays and even went to confession. But because they had never been explained to her, the rituals remained a mystery. She never knew what was being said or how the words related to her life and behavior. She simply went along with everything because she knew she would be punished if she did not. As she grew older, Miriam began to hate anything connected with Catholicism, for it seemed to her a system of arbitrary punishments. Now in her thirties, Miriam believes she might have appreciated the moral guidance and spiritual sustenance she could have gained through Catholicism had she known it was available. Not until she went to college and began to read about religion on her own did she understand the meaning Catholicism could have had for her life.

This anecdote is not meant to imply that a knowledge of right and wrong is synonymous with a religious education. What it does illustrate is that moral attitudes and matters of spirit and conscience are sources of confusion to children who do not receive guidance on such matters from their parents. Deaf children can easily live within a system of right and wrong without discerning it. Thus, here again, the rule to be explicit applies.

THE SIGNIFICANCE OF PLAY

This chapter has covered some weighty topics—from communication to morality. The responsibilities and considerations involved in raising a deaf child must, by their sheer numbers alone, seem imposing at first. But it is important that you do not face this task grimly. Clearly, raising any child entails work. Raising a deaf child means more work still. But the word *work* applies only in the sense that there is much to be accomplished. As for *how* the job is to be done, the method could, and should, involve a large measure of play.

For very young children work and play are identical. It is parents and teachers who have a way of distinguishing between the two. Unfortunately, children usually learn early that work is what you are *supposed* to do, that it is usually no fun, and that it makes you tired. Play, on the other hand, is what you are allowed to do in reward for performing work. But for preschool children of three and four, their play *is* their work. Through fantasy, interaction with their playmates, and story telling, they build and cement their knowledge of the world.

What is true for hearing children in this context is true for deaf children. Both learn through playing, pretending, and imagining. Both discover things about the world through freely exploring on their own. Both remember an idea they have stumbled on during play long after they have forgotten a windy explanation or a tiresome demonstration.

And though it does not always follow, in this case what is true for the children is often true for the adults. A game, a story, even a messy try at making pancakes together, might ease the strain of your responsibilities in ways that a serious attempt at teaching your child to share toys would not. Making a game of button-sorting or coloring might teach color discrimination faster than a lesson after dinner when everyone is tired. Even the frustration of blocked communication can be lightened by an old-fashioned game of charades once the child is five or six. The added advantage of such activities is that they involve the whole family, giving you a chance to share the burden of total attentiveness. In time, perhaps, the distinction between work and play will fade for you as well, as you and your deaf child explore and learn together.

Chapter 3

Nonverbal Communication

WE RISK STATING THE OBVIOUS by defining deafness once more.

Your child has a hearing impairment that may be compensated for to some extent but will never be corrected. To one degree or another, your child cannot and never will hear.

If the child has been deaf from birth, it is likely that he or she will not, or has not, learned to speak by the age at which hearing children normally acquire language. Your child will probably eventually learn to speak but will always experience some degree of difficulty in understanding others and in being understood. Simply put, speaking and understanding speech will always be more complex for a deaf child than for a hearing child of the same age.

In these two areas, then—that of comprehending spoken language and of speaking itself—lie the major limitations the deaf child faces in life. These are formidable problems in a world that takes hearing and speaking for granted.

But notice: Deafness affects hearing and speech, *not* the impulse to communicate. Your deaf child has as great a desire and as great a need to transmit and receive information as anyone else. Furthermore, deafness affects hearing and, by extension, speech, but it does not rob the body of the power to communicate. Deaf people still have their hands and arms, their faces, their postures, their gestures, their expressions, their lips, and their tongues. And they have their eyes: They can read the gestures, postures, expressions, and often the speech of others. True, spoken language is the natural medium for communication among human beings. The focus here on the importance of nonverbal communication is in no way intended to undervalue speech or to dismiss the seriousness of deafness as a disability. But in truth, hearing people often *over-value* speech as a means of transmitting information by considering it the *only* such means. They are surprised to learn that, according to various empirical studies, a large percentage of normal social conversation among *hearing* people is *nonverbal* in nature. That is, a small portion of the total energy used in communicating is expended in the utterance of words.

Many people are surprised to learn that deaf people watch television and go to the movies. How can you tell what's going on? they ask. How can you follow the plot? But most television shows, especially those that tell stories, show people in action. Everything in these shows, not just the script, is designed to communicate information relevant to the story: costumes, sets, pace, and, of course, the gestures, expressions, and postures of the actors. People who are used to scanning the visual world for information have no trouble following a story on TV. Significantly, deaf people can watch action-oriented TV programs without missing much, but hearing people *cannot* usually follow a TV program without the sound on. Hearing people are so used to relying on speech as their chief source of information that they are less adept at gathering information visually.

Hearing people do transmit and read body language, but for the most part they do so subconsciously. Consciously, when they engage in conversation or watch a TV program or a movie, they focus on the spoken words. Whatever information they pick up through their other senses is recorded subliminally (that is, outside the area of conscious awareness). For example, you might ask your friend how he's feeling today and hear him say he's fine, just fine. You walk away thinking, "Well, I'm glad Joe's fine," but still have a nagging feeling that something was wrong with him, that somehow he was not telling you the truth. If you were to see a videotape of the exchange, you might notice that throughout your conversation Joe's eyes kept darting elsewhere and he pulled at his tie as if it were choking him. Since Joe is an unusually direct fellow, you would recognize that his darting eyes had a message of their own, and you might interpret his tie-pulling gesture as a symbol for Joe's choking on a lie. But because you are used to accepting Joe's word, you dismiss your nagging feelings, having had difficulty explaining to yourself why you had them at all. A deaf person experienced in consciously observing body language, however, might be more prepared to treat the eye darting and tie pulling as part of Joe's message. He or she might perceive right away that Joe felt terrible, despite what he said.

Depending on speech is like relying on a car for getting around. You drive everywhere rather than walking, and though you get where you want to go quickly and efficiently, you soon grow lazy and out of shape. Your child's deafness should serve to motivate you to learn to use your body again. You will need to sharpen your perceptions about gesture, posture, and facial expression and to loosen up and use these elements when communicating with your child.

The rest of this chapter is about the role nonverbal communication can play in your interactions with your deaf child. The first section has to do with the child's potential to communicate nonverbally, a potential that is inborn and only waiting to be encouraged and nurtured. The second section focuses on ways in which you can develop your own body language in communicating with your deaf child.

THE BODY LANGUAGE OF CHILDREN

Jean Piaget, the great developmental psychologist, described children's first communication experiences with others as "acted conversations."* Such exchanges consist of bobbing, shoving, pointing, pushing, punching, and waving. The messages involved may seem cryptic at times, but more often than not preverbal children manage to get their points across. Thus, even when observing hearing children, we must shed the common misconception that nonverbal communication is not *real* communication.

Consider the following scenario. Two ten-month-old children sit side by side in a sandbox. Both are absorbed in filling their own brightly colored cups with sand. Suddenly the little boy glances up, notices the girl's red cup, drops his own yellow cup and brushes it aside impatiently, and then reaches out to take a firm grip on the red one. Simultaneously with this series of actions, the boy's facial expressions register delighted interest as he spies the red cup, impatience as he casts his own cup aside, and knit-browed determination as he fastens his grip on the rim of the red one. A struggle ensues—a tug-of-war, really—and as the little girl loses her grip on the prize, her moan of irritation grows into a high-pitched shriek of fury. In a flash, she quits her screeching to lean over and savagely bite the cheek of the interloper. He lets go of the cup and begins his own wail of pain and surprise. As the scene closes, the chastened boy is stretching out his arms to his mommy, and the girl, having prudently turned her back to the boy, is once more tranquilly engaged in filling her red cup with sand.

Who is to say communication has not occurred here? True, these two hearing children are too young to manipulate language to their own ends. Ten-month-old babies understand many words and even say a few, but as to getting their points across they are basically nonverbal. Nevertheless, the primitive state of their language development has not prevented these two from making their feelings about their cups quite clear. These two babies expressed a whole range of feelings—happy

---

*H. Ginsberg and O. Opper, *Piaget's Theory of Intellectual Development: An Introduction* (Englewood Cliffs, N.J.: Prentice-Hall, 1969), p. 221.

desire, determined acquisitiveness, fury, hurt—and even suggested a few abstract concepts—possessiveness, territoriality, smug satisfaction—all without language. Furthermore, their meanings were not just restricted to themselves but were clearly understandable to observers.

Dr. Katherine Bridges, a child psychologist, discovered in her research with normally hearing children that by age two years, regardless of their background or sex, children are capable of communicating nonverbally a total of twelve different emotions. The emotions they convey include elation, affection, excitement, anger, jealousy, joy, distress, delight, fear, and so on.*

"But wait a minute," you might object. "Is conveying feelings really communicating? Isn't real communication concerned with information?"

In fact, a great proportion of the messages we send have to do with our feelings. Where children are concerned, it is fair to say that the majority of their messages have to do with how they feel. To test this statement, survey the content of the communication that passes between you and a hearing child, perhaps another child in your family or someone you spend time with. Or consider the following example, a verbatim transcription of a typical morning conversation between a mother and her three-year-old son:

"Good morning. How are you feeling today? Did you sleep well?"

"Mommy, I'm hungry."

"What would you like for breakfast? How about some eggs?"

"Yuck, I *hate* eggs. Let me have some um, uh, um—you

---

*See Barbara S. Wood, *Children and Communication: Verbal and Nonverbal Language Development* (Englewood Cliffs, N.J.: Prentice-Hall, Inc., 1976), pp. 193–195.

know what? Jason at school said I was a dumdum and I cried."

"Oh, that's awful. But you're not a dumdum. Did you tell him you weren't? Calling names is terrible. Now, what do you want for breakfast?"

"I'm not hungry."

"But you have to eat. Otherwise you'll be too hungry when you get to school."

"But I don't want to go to school! I want you to stay home and let me stay home with you!"

"But I thought you *loved* school! Why don't you want to go to school? I think you'll feel better about it when you have something to eat. What do you want for breakfast?"

"I don't *want* any breakfast. I *hate* breakfast."

The content of this conversation is almost totally emotional—how I feel, what I want or don't want, and so on. Much of what children talk about, and much of what they need to get across to their parents and others, has to do with their feelings. Thus, to deny the importance of the emotions children communicate is to deny the importance of the subject matter of greatest significance to them.

Of course, most parents do respond to their babies' expressive motions. But most do not treat such movements as valuable bearers of information. They take pleasure in the expressions and gestures their babies make but often think of the children as noncommunicative until they learn to talk. The parent of a deaf child, however, has a special reason to concentrate hard on the vocabulary of gestures, expressions, and postures that the child develops over time. By learning to read the child's body language, the parent comes a step closer to participating in an ongoing conversation every bit as valid and informative as a verbal exchange.

Eventually you and your child may develop a system of signs and signals that you agree upon together. But for the moment don't worry about trying to *teach* your child sign language. Concentrate on the child's natural movements and expressions. After all, as far as your child is concerned, communicating with gestures and facial expressions and investing postures with meaning are what communication is all about. Until the child is three or four and begins to realize that he or she is different from others, deafness is simply the way things are. Nothing is *missing* from the child's world from his or her point of view. Hearing is inconceivable to the baby. The child is prepared to go along as she or he has been since birth, communicating through body movement, facial expression, and posture.

Given children's natural talent for nonverbal communication, it is doubly sad that many parents simply do not perceive their children's efforts to express themselves. Though the children persist in the only way they know—and in a way that has great potential for conveying information—all too often their parents remain unaware of their efforts, let alone of how effective the gestures could be were the parents to learn to decode them. Unfortunately, this situation is very common among the families of deaf children. Many parents with deaf children remain totally unaware of their children's nonverbal communication skills altogether. Sometimes this ignorance is a manifestation of the parents' intense wish that their child be normal, that old self-deception: "If he could only learn to speak, he wouldn't be deaf anymore." In their single-minded hope that the child may learn to speak, such parents focus on the spoken mode of expression to the total exclusion of other modes. "Learn to talk, learn to talk" is the message they send. Very often, what they are really saying, though perhaps subconsciously, is "Forget about other ways of communicating. Just learn to talk."

One common situation clearly exemplifies this approach and its effect on a deaf child. Imagine that four-year-old Marie has lost her ball somewhere in the house. She goes to her parents, who are talking together in another room, and begins gesturing for them to come help her look for her ball. "What is it?" her father asks. "I think she's lost something. What are you looking for, Marie?" her mother asks, enunciating carefully. The girl begins to gesture excitedly again, but her parents are still unable to tell what she is looking for. Stumped, they look at each other and exchange a puzzled glance, and then the father loses his temper. In the past, he has had some success in teaching the girl to form certain words, and he is furious that now when she really needs to communicate information, she relies totally on gestures, a code he has been unable to crack. "Come back when you can tell us what you're looking for," he shouts angrily and turns his back on the girl.

Having failed to get her message across, failed to enlist her parents' help, and failed to find her ball, Marie's frustration is building to a full-blown tantrum. But much worse for her than the momentary frustration is the confusion she experiences regarding the meaning of her father's reaction. Why is he angry? Because he doesn't understand me? Because I was gesturing? Because he has no time to help me? Does it mean that gestures are always unacceptable? Does it mean that he doesn't love me?

The last question might seem extreme, especially to parents who want only the best for their children and who make their rules—such as "Learn language; don't gesture"—out of love and concern for the child's well-being. But consider: How would you feel if someone you felt close to—a relative, say, from another country—suddenly burst out in fury, "Don't talk to me in English, ever! Learn to speak my language or don't speak to me again!" You might easily conclude that you weren't very well thought of, since surely a person who cared for you would make an effort to meet you halfway. You might interpret the rebuff as total rejection, and with reason.

Such misunderstanding can shatter a child's feelings of security early in life. To grow strong and independent, a child needs to feel totally accepted. As shown, the danger, where a deaf child is concerned, is that the parents will unknowingly threaten that sense of security by making their love and acceptance conditional on the child's learning to communicate formally, through speech or sign language. Children whose nonverbal efforts at communicating are devalued and who are discouraged from making them may come to feel that only when they learn the art of verbal communication will their parents truly love and accept them fully.

A parent guarding against that danger and attempting to take advantage of the child's natural skills at nonverbal communication would react very differently from Marie's father when confronted with the lost-ball situation. Instead of brushing aside the child's attempts to explain the problem, both parents would enter into a guessing game—gesturing, speaking, questioning, following hunches—until the problem was identified. Then they would start looking for the ball along with the child. The child would have conveyed the problem and in doing so would have involved the parents in the solution. The function of communication, at least in this particular situation, would have been achieved, and the child would have experienced the satisfaction of having initiated a successful exchange, whether or not the ball was found. Above all, the child would feel proof of the parents' interest and concern and would have no reason to question their love.

The common impulse among parents of deaf children to discourage the use of body language in favor of verbal communication has another serious consequence: it inhibits children's natural impulse to learn as much as possible about their environment and their own place in it. Observe a hearing two-year-old and you will realize how much simple body motion means to that child in terms of being alive and participating in the world. Babies do not sit still passively in the middle of a room or a landscape. They roam, feel, seek boundaries, feel textures. They look at people, coo at them, crawl to them, and touch them. From a child's point of view, living and existing are synonymous with moving and reaching out.

Deaf children, of course, have as much need to be physically free as hearing children—perhaps more, since they have one less sense through which to receive information about the world. Therefore, unless discouraged, the deaf child will move, move, move—seeking knowledge of the world and stimulation for his or her active senses. And later, at the point at which the hearing child starts to give up some of the motor activity in favor of verbal communication, the deaf child will continue to use bodily movement as a mode of expression and a means of eliciting responses. At the same time, while the hearing child grows less bodily oriented, the movements of the deaf child at about age four or five become more refined, more subtle, and more capable of conveying specific meanings.

In summary, then, although your child is deaf, he or she is not without language. The vocabulary of this language consists of blinks, nods, sweeping arm movements, tiny finger movements, wrinklings of the nose, barings of the teeth, changing angles of the head, specific attitudes of the spine—in short, an infinity of gestures, expressions, and postures. This self-evolved body language will never be as precise and explicit as verbal language. You will have to sharpen your sensitivity to learn to read it, and even then interpreting it will give you many moments of confusion and frustration. But as long as you try, you will be confirming the value of your child's attempts to reach you and to let you know what is going on inside. Failing to learn the body language of preschool deaf children is to plug your ears to the messages they are sending. To discover how much your deaf child has to say, open your eyes!

DEVELOPING YOUR OWN BODY LANGUAGE

We have talked of being receptive to your child's body-language messages. The other half of the communication process is, of course, transmitting messages. The focus of this section is on your role in a nonverbal exchange.

As noted earlier, many hearing people are so dependent on speech that they fail to recognize how important body language is in their own lives. Perhaps the easiest way of realizing the significance of body language is to imagine an exchange without it. Visualize a meeting with a very old, dear friend whom you have not seen in years. Can you imagine greeting this person in words alone, without at the very least breaking into a happy smile and extending your hand in greeting? In fact, you would probably make a great many more movements, depending on how expressive a person you are naturally, and you would probably be unaware of most of them. But were you to greet this long lost friend merely by speaking, even while raising your voice to indicate your excitement, it is possible your friend might read your reception as a snub. "Hmm. No handshake? No smile? Just standing there with his hands at his sides? He must not be very glad to see me," the friend might conclude.

In fact, such a scenario is unlikely, since our eye movements, most of which are outside our conscious controls, communicate messages of excitement, arousal, pleasure, grief, sorrow, and so on. Truly, the eyes, as the poet said, are the windows to the soul. The shades of meaning conveyed by the eyes can be extremely subtle. For example, research has shown that when a man is shown a picture of a beautiful woman his pupils may dilate to twice their normal size. Thus, although a man may be unaware that he is giving himself away, observers might see his interest by consciously or unconsciously noting the dilation of his pupils.

Given this degree of expressiveness, for a deaf child your eyes can be an important source of information. Thus, it is important to maintain eye contact at all times when communicating with your deaf child. Otherwise you will be withholding the visual equivalent of the tone of your voice. If you make it difficult for the child to read your eyes, he or she might get the gist of your message without gaining a sense of your personal feelings on the matter. In cases where the parents consistently fail to meet the eyes of their deaf children, the latter have no means of detecting their parents' mood. In extreme cases, the children might feel they do not really know their parents at all.

Verbal Supremacy: A Fallacy

Sadly, the same impulse that leads parents to discourage the use of body language in their deaf children—the desire to make them concentrate on verbal skills—very often leads them to suppress their own body language. So intent are these well-meaning parents on helping their deaf children acquire language skills that they suppress all facial expressions and gestures and deprive their children of physical clues to the meaning of their verbal messages. They do not want to distract their child's attention from *words*. They forget, or do not know, that by stripping away their body language they are stripping away a large percentage of the content of normal social conversation. Ironically, they leave their deaf children—who need all the clues they can get—with only 20 percent or less of the communication tools available to hearing people. Thus a very common complaint among deaf people with hearing siblings is that their parents were generally *more* expressive with the hearing children in the family than with the deaf children.

Nonverbal communication does not *replace* speech or sign language. Rather, it supplements other modes of communication. Since most deaf children learn language much later than their normal hearing peers, they need to be encouraged to develop other modes of conveying and receiving information. Communication feeds curiosity and sparks self-awareness. To delay a child's ability to communicate until the child can learn language is to risk inhibiting the development of these very basic qualities.

Getting Your Message Straight

If you have relied on speech as the primary vehicle of communication all your life, you might have to become newly acquainted with your own body and its potential for transmitting messages. You might literally have to spend time in front of a mirror to determine what messages you are sending and to devise gestures and expressions to match your messages.

Specific Techniques

Body language is not a complex system that has to be studied and learned. In fact, as you will doubtless notice in the table of translations on pages 70–75, the meanings of specific facial expressions and physical gestures are fairly universal, at least within a given culture. Therefore, the point of focusing on specific techniques is not to teach you body language but only to help you to make conscious your understanding and your use of it. Nevertheless, some special points about using body language do arise with respect to deaf children.

1. A very important but obvious reminder: Be sure to perform your gestures and use your facial expressions on a level with the child's eye. It does no good to shake your head and scowl strongly to mean "No!" if you are standing at your full height far above the child's line of sight. Kneel down and make direct eye contact with the child before you begin trying to get your point across.

2. Remember that all eye cues are important and that they carry the subtler aspects of your message. For this reason, too, maintain eye contact at all times. Stay conscious of your head movements and make it as easy as possible for the child to see your eyes.

3. Be as responsive as possible with your face and body to all your child's messages. Do not restrict your use of body language to the very active, message-sending function of communication. Remember that the child misses out on the sounds people ordinarily make in encouraging a speaker to continue. Without visual cues to encourage them, deaf children have no way of knowing whether their listeners are still interested and engaged.

4. Use *normal* gestures as much as possible. Neither restrict nor exaggerate your gestures and expressions. Be aware that it is through you that the child will learn how gestures and expressions are used among hearing people generally. By using the common vocabulary of body language, you will be helping your child to read the gestures of others and to send nonverbal messages that will be understood by others.

5. As your child grows older, be prepared to refine your body language and use it at a more sophisticated level. The older the child, the subtler and more complex will be the meanings conveyed nonverbally.

6. Be alert to the fact that every deaf child becomes a mimic at one period in early childhood. This phase usually occurs between ages three and five, once the child learns to understand others and realizes that he or she can get messages across. At this point, the child is excited by the newfound power to communicate and starts imitating and repeating every gesture that evokes a response. Again, during this period parents commonly fear that the child's attachment to gestures is too wholehearted and exclusive. Be reassured that the phase represents a passing enchantment with the power of the newly mastered communication tool. It is analogous to hearing children's fascination with the telephone and is bound to pass as the novelty wears off. Following this phase, body language functions as a supplement to the other methods of communication introduced to the child.

Translations

The following is a table of common phrases and their renderings in body language. The purpose of this list is not to teach you how to convey a sentence nonverbally word by word but to show by example that body language is natural and that most messages are instantly recognizable to most people. Because children are able to handle more complex messages as they grow older, the list is roughly broken into groups by age. But these demarcations are meant as approximations only. Every child will show a different aptitude for understanding and sending messages at various levels of complexity.

AGE TWO

PHRASE	TRANSLATION
"Open your mouth."	Simply open your mouth and point to your open mouth,

holding your face directly in front of your child's. In all nonverbal exchanges, take advantage of your child's natural urge to imitate your expressions and gestures.

"Are you sleepy?"

Show your droopy eyes, yawn, furrow your brow in an interrogatory way, and then point to the child. The child will soon learn that a querying expression coupled with a pointed finger means that a response is expected.

"Are you hungry?"

Pretend to chew, rub your stomach, smile, query with your brow, and point to the child.

"What's wrong?"

Show a worried face by frowning and looking at the child intently. Place your hand on the child and incline your body toward him or her in concern. Then with your face query and point with your finger.

"Good girl!"

Smile and look pleased. Touch or point to the child to make sure she understands that she is the cause of your pleasure. Let your whole body—arms, shoulders, back—show your pleasure.

"No! That was very bad."

Look very displeased and shake your head from side to side. Hold your head, neck, and back rigid. The child will soon learn to associate a side-to-side shake with "no" and up-and-down with "yes," just as hearing children do. As you shake your head, touch the child or point to the child to make it clear that he or she has caused your disapproval. Simultaneously indicate what *exactly* the child has done wrong. Act out the misbehavior if necessary.

AGES TWO TO FOUR

"Go to your room!"

Point to the room, then point to the child. Make a gesture of "no" if the child begins to lose interest or do something else. Be firm and do not smile. Relaxing your posture will undermine your intention.

"Go to the bathroom."

Same as above, but not angrily. May be necessary to point to the appropriate areas on your body and query the child.

"What are you doing?"

Query the child with your facial expression, shrug a little, and point to the activity in question. Be sure to remain attentive after you have invited the response.

"Where are you going?"

Incline your head a little to show direction, query the child with your facial expression, and point to the child.

"Tie your shoes."

Make a tying motion with your fingers and point to the child's shoes. This may seem too obvious an example to mention, but parents often tend to mouth commands and look or point at the *child,* leaving the child to guess what is being requested.

"One, two, three, *go!*"

Translate the tag lines to games into body language. In this case, count off the steps on your fingers, raise your eyebrows, brighten up your expression, and move hands forward for "Go!"

"Good! It's delicious. Do you think so?"

You should be able to discuss the qualities of things by this time. Show your enjoyment of the dish at hand. Then point to the child and query.

"Oh, what a terrible cake."

Roll your eyes and show disgust. Hold your nose if you have to.

AGES FOUR TO FIVE

"Let's go to a movie."

In making plans, you should work on conveying your attitude toward what you are saying. You could say "Let's go to a movie" verbally in a way that would communicate ambivalence, excitement, boredom, or uncertainty. First work on getting the concept "movie" across. This might take some charades. Then work on the subjective side of the question, eliciting the child's opinion with a query and a point.

"Oh, you silly thing! *You* do the whole job then!"

Humor should be a solid part of your nonverbal repertoire by now. Up to age three or four, there is always some danger in interjecting sarcasm or irony, since the child might take it literally. But now you should be able to risk light name-calling with affectionate intent. In this case, you could look angry and kind at the same time and give a gentle shove toward the job to be done, crossing your arms and turning away from it.

"Which one do *you* want? I'd like that one."

Show the options, show your preference, query the child with your expression, and point to both the choices and

the child. Then be prepared to
negotiate.

As mentioned, the level of complexity and subtlety of nonverbal communication continues to increase with age. Furthermore, other modes of communication as the child learns them
open up the nonverbal level even further, since nonverbal techniques combined with more precise methods lend depth to the
message. One personal memory recalls for Paul the complexity
of the information that can be carried by nonverbal means.
When he was about twelve years old, his brother took him to
the airport to meet their parents on an incoming flight. While
waiting for the plane, the brother sat across from a row of
doorless telephone booths, all for the moment occupied. As
Paul scanned the line of men talking on the phone, he could
tell which men were enjoying their conversations and which
were not, which were talking with people they liked or loved
and which with strangers or business associates, which were
nervous about what they were saying and which were talking
naturally. He could even speculate about which men were ly-
ing and which were telling the truth. How much more could
he have learned about those men if they had been talking to
Paul himself while he maintained the same level of alertness to
their nonverbal signals?

Consistency and Straightforwardness
Your goal in training yourself to communicate physically
will be to send clear, consistent messages that cannot be misin-
terpreted. Consistency is an important area of concern for the
parents of deaf children, since confusion is inevitable when the
body and the intended message contradict each other. Sometimes, when we are not in total control of our bodies or when
we feel ambivalence, our body movements can be inconsistent
with the message we are trying to convey. Thus, the child
might think, "His body is saying OK but his gestures are saying no," or "His gestures are saying you did well but his eyes

are saying you weren't good enough." Or in the case of a child who can speechread, "His mouth is telling me to go ahead but his eyes are saying stay here."

It might be asking a lot to expect a parent to be 100 percent consistent. But you can learn to eliminate common sources of confusion that arise when your body comes into conflict with your message. For example, when your preschooler has a furious temper tantrum in the middle of the grocery store and hundreds of eyes are turned your way, you might be tempted to smile and subdue your angry gestures as you try to make it clear to the child that his behavior is totally unacceptable. Thus, you will wind up smiling as you say or gesture, "You bad, bad boy," and your child will wonder what you really mean. You might eliminate the inevitable subsequent tantrums by ignoring the eyes of the world and making it very clear, with no softening expression or gesture, that such behavior will not be tolerated again. Remember, the child will not be sophisticated enough to realize that you are embarrassed. He or she will expect you to mean what you say. If your meaning is unclear due to your own indirectness, the child, at a disadvantage, becomes a victim of your own lack of straightforwardness.

On the other hand, though your child, like all children, will be unable to sort out all mixed messages, do not underestimate his or her ability to read your body language. Remember, the child has been reading your expressions, gestures, and postures all along and has become well versed in their meanings. Particularly when you first discover that your child is deaf, you might feel the need to lie, to pretend all is well, and to conceal your shock, guilt, or denial from the child. Do not fool yourself into thinking you can hide your true feelings by smiling and patting your child on the head. The child will be able to read your unhappiness and will need reassurance, as any child needs reassurance when he or she perceives his parents, his Rock of Gibraltar, to be in danger of crumbling. The challenge here is to acknowledge your feelings and at the same time protect your child's sense of security.

PEOPLE-WATCHING

One more hint on body language came to Paul by way of his father, who had the knack of reading the gestures of unknown people. He would point out people to Paul, saying, "Look at that woman with her arms folded across her chest. She will never give in. She's protecting her position" or "Do you see how that man clings to the arm of that woman over there? He has staked his claim for the world to see. But she's looking off toward the great unknown."

Paul's parents and brothers often took him people-watching when he was a child—at least that is what Paul thought they were doing on their many excursions. The family would stroll along and just watch people interacting with each other, and Paul's parents or brothers would provide commentary and show him what to look for. Thinking back, Paul realizes his family revealed their personalities according to what they described and what they found interesting. The boys covered a whole range of people, his father was interested in families, and his mother, though ordinarily the most careful to fill the boy in on what was happening minute by minute, showed a ladylike reticence in her failing to mention certain goings-on between the men and women they passed.

Paul remembers very clearly an incident that took place when he was nine years old, on one of these outings with an older brother. The boys were sitting on a bench in a park in New York City. Nearby, a small boy was eating candy. As they watched, the boy's sister, slightly older, approached him and demanded a share. He refused quietly and went on eating. His calm stubbornness enraged the little girl, and she hit him, yelled, stamped off, returned, but all to no avail. The boy finished his candy and began to play in the sandbox. Paul and his brother stayed where they were for a long while after that, just watching. Every so often the girl came back to harrass her brother—talking sharply to him, kicking down a structure he had made in the sand, making a mean face at him. Paul realized then that people's gestures and messages to each other were not always related to the matters at hand. Some things were carry-overs from unresolved arguments, like the one they had been observing, or other conversations or exchanges that had taken place in the past. This insight represented a big jump in Paul's understanding of the way people communicated with each other. He was able to see that relationships between people are infinitely complex and often unfathomable, even for hearing observers.

This example demonstrates how much there is to learn about human communication, and how much deaf children *can* learn if their parents encourage them and show them how to observe. One need not be rude to "eavesdrop" on gestures, only receptive. For the shy, movies and television offer a feast of body language for the deaf child to study—and for the parents of the deaf child to learn from, too.

In conclusion, it is important to stress that encouraging your deaf child to communicate nonverbally will *not* make him or her lose interest in learning other modes of communication. Nonverbal communication supplements other modes, helping deaf children take part in the flow of ideas so necessary to their growth and development. In those early years, communication in whatever form feeds the mind. How can we deny our deaf children the right to learn and grow? And how can we deny ourselves the chance to get to know these children as individuals at the earliest opportunity? By silencing the language of gesture, we isolate our deaf children and ourselves from each other. In communication, of whatever form, everyone gains.

Chapter 4

Modes of Communication

THE MEANINGS OF MANY of the words used in this chapter may seem quite obvious at first. But ask yourself: Are you really sure of the differences between, for example, *speech* and *language*? or between *communication* and *speech*? Definitions of such familiar words tend to get blurred in daily life, but in making decisions about your deaf child's mode of communication, you will need to sharpen these definitions in your mind so you can follow the arguments and weigh pros and cons.

Furthermore, you'll need to determine how others use particular terms and labels, since even professionals in the field of deafness often use the same words to mean different things, or different words to mean the same things. What one teacher means by the oral method might be what another refers to as the aural-oral method. What one means by total communication another might call the simultaneous method. Therefore, we begin this chapter with a glossary of terms to help you find your way through this maze. Here, the terms are defined as briefly as possible, with the emphasis given to features that distinguish them. In the text, we describe in detail each method cited in this list.

GLOSSARY

COMMUNICATION: Interaction that conveys information among living creatures. For humans, the expression of feelings and ideas and the reception of others' feelings and ideas.

LANGUAGE: A systematic means of communicating feelings and ideas by use of signs, sounds, gestures, or marks having meanings understood by a considerable group.

SPEECH: Communication in audible language via the mouth, tongue, voice box, and breath.

GESTURES: Body movements used to communicate feelings or ideas.

SIGNS: Symbols formed by the hands to communicate letters, parts of words, words, or concepts.

AMERICAN SIGN LANGUAGE (ASL, AMESLAN): A sign language distinct from English that is the native language of many American deaf people.

SIGNED ENGLISH (MANUALLY CODED ENGLISH): A system of signs that serves as a code for English and thus as a means of communicating manually in English, as opposed to ASL.

SEEING ESSENTIAL ENGLISH (SEE I): One system of signed English.

SIGNING EXACT ENGLISH (SEE II): Another system of signed English.

LINGUISTICS OF VISUAL ENGLISH (LOVE): Another system of signed English.

PIDGIN SIGN ENGLISH: A language composed of both ASL and English that differs according to the users' knowledge; where the English user knows little ASL the language contains more English, but the more ASL the English user knows the more Pidgin Sign English resembles ASL.

SIGN LANGUAGES: Standardized systems of signs for communication, each system having its own vocabulary, rules, and usages, not necessarily corresponding to those in the society's native spoken language.

FINGERSPELLING: The spelling of words with the fingers by means of manual symbols representing letters in the alphabet.

LIPREADING: Receiving the meaning of speech by translating the movements of the speaker's lips.

SPEECHREADING: Receiving the meaning of speech by translating the movement of the speaker's lips, tongue, and face, and related body postures and gestures.

RESIDUAL HEARING: The hearing, if any, that exists in a hearing-impaired person.

AUDITORY TRAINING: The teaching of hearing-impaired people to use their residual hearing.

AMPLIFICATION: Increasing by means of hearing aids or auditory trainers the loudness of the sounds available to hearing-impaired people through their residual hearing.

ORAL METHOD (ORALISM): An education method based on the belief that the main goal in educating deaf children is to teach them to speak and to speechread. Children taught by the oral method are generally not permitted to use sign language in their formal educational process.

MANUAL METHODS (MANUALISM): The exclusive use of sign language in the education of the deaf, with no attention given to speech. No pure manual programs exist in the United States today.

TOTAL COMMUNICATION (TC): The combination of oralism, manualism, auditory training, and visual aids. The degree to which each mode is stressed depends on the particular child.

AUDITORY METHOD (UNISENSORY METHOD): Training to enable children to develop their listening skills by relying primarily on hearing.

AURAL-ORAL METHOD: Oralism combined with auditory training and amplification.

ROCHESTER METHOD (A SIMULTANEOUS METHOD): Oralism combined with fingerspelling.

CUED SPEECH: Oralism combined with a limited number of hand shapes representing phonetic units.

THE OLD CONTROVERSY: ORALISM VERSUS TOTAL COMMUNICATION

The best method for educating the deaf has been the subject of fierce controversy for as long as the need for special techniques has been acknowledged. The conflict has taken many forms over time and, as we will show, involves many interrelated issues. But the fundamental debate has been between pure oralists—those who believe the deaf should learn to communicate through speech and lipreading alone—and those who advocate various degrees of manualism. Because research has never proved either method to be clearly superior, the battle rages on. In our own time, the two camps are composed of oralists and supporters of total communication, which, most basically, is the *combined* use of speech auditory training, sign language, fingerspelling, and visual aids.

Often, when parents are poorly informed about this controversy, they tend to follow the advice of the first professional they encounter, unaware that alternatives exist that might better meet their children's particular needs. It is our goal in this chapter to explain the controversy and the alternatives as fully as possible while still remaining objective. This approach is based on our belief, expressed throughout the book, that deciding how your deaf child is to communicate, at least initially, should be up to you, and not up to the doctors, audiologists, counselors, or educators who advise you. The role of these professional people is just that—to *advise.* Your family alone will live with the decision you make, and your child will gain or suffer by it.

The reason for worrying about who is responsible for the decision—and the reason the methods controversy has raged on for so long—is that no method of educating deaf children is perfect. Inevitably, no matter which course you choose, you will have moments, weeks, or months of uncertainty and doubt. Even more basic is that original lesson, which, it seems, must be learned time and again: Whichever method you choose, your child will remain deaf, and whichever method you choose, your child will experience communication difficulties throughout life.

That said, let us turn to the controversy as it presents itself in our time, and to what it can teach about the available options.

The Central Issue

The central issue is simple enough: Should deaf children be permitted to use sign language or not?

In our modern version of the controversy, two conflicting groups emerge around this issue:

(1) *the oralists,* who argue that learning speech is the right of all deaf children, that without speech deaf people remain isolated from the society, and that sign language should be prohibited because it interferes with deaf children's acquisition of speech skills. Simply put, the oralist argument is that sign language will either distract deaf children from learning speech or, because it is easier to learn, kill what motivation deaf students have to learn speech.

(2) *the proponents of total communication,* who believe that learning sign language is the right of all deaf children. They argue that a child may require years to attain good speech and speechreading (if he or she learns them at all), whereas a child can learn sign language much more quickly and easily, thus acquiring the ability to communicate from an early age.

Although the debate centers on methods of education and classroom learning, the decision on methods will have lifelong consequences for the child. One might argue that the mode of communication affects every aspect of a person's life. Thus, to illustrate the consequences of this decision, we turn first to what we call the issue's "cultural aspect."

Oralism versus Total Communication: The Cultural Aspect

More and more deaf people think of the deaf and the hearing as inhabiting two separate worlds, usually referred to as the deaf and hearing worlds. These worlds have separate cultures and distinct languages. The hearing world is dominated by speech, the deaf by sign language. Those holding this view see the communication problems that arise between deaf and hearing people as analogous to those that divide any two groups of people with different native languages. We can use this analogy to clarify the oralist-totalist controversy as it relates to the world outside the classroom.

Oralists argue that in order to understand and participate in hearing culture, deaf people must grow up learning the communication mode of the hearing, in our case spoken English. They feel that without the opportunity to gain this tool deaf people are prevented from benefiting from and participating in society. Proponents of total communication retort by accusing nonsigning oralists of denying their identity as natives of the deaf world, and of vainly trying to assume the identity of hearing people. "You may be able to imitate a hearing person temporarily," a totalist might argue. "But whenever hearing people turn their backs on you, you will be deaf again." Totalists feel that sign language not only facilitates speech and speechreading development, but that it links deaf people together, enabling them to feel socially and emotionally accepted as a group by the society. The forging of a group identity in turn, totalists argue, helps members to accept their deafness more easily, for they can view it as a shared characteristic.

In trying to decide between an oral and a TC program, you should be familiar with these ways of thinking about deafness. What are your own feelings about cultural identity? Do you see oralism's prohibition against sign language as a wall between your child and the people he or she might feel most at home with? Or do you see the goal of education as helping your child to leave the deaf world and to participate fully in the hearing world? Or is your intention to provide your child with the tools for moving freely between both worlds? These are the crucial questions you will answer in selecting the mode of communication your child will learn in school.

In the case histories that follow, the results of two very different "oral successes" are explored with regard to these cultural considerations. In the end, these sketches are merely the stories of two people. We point to no moral and reach no conclusions. Again, we present the dilemma but leave the solution to you.

John

John's parents had high ambitions for all five of their children, and John's profound deafness did not alter their faith in education as the road to professional success. In deciding on a course of education, initially John's parents were more concerned about the academic levels rather than the philosophies of the schools they considered. Eventually, they chose a new and vigorous oral program at a private school in a neighboring county. John entered the school at age five and stayed through the eighth grade. In his freshman year of high school, he entered his local public school.

Students at John's oral school were not allowed to use sign language, homemade signs, or gestures under any circumstances. Even when they were tempted to use their hands in conversation as a hearing person might—as in "the fish was this big"—they were required to use speech instead. And the no-signing rule applied not only to the classrooms but to the playground and social rooms as well. From John's first day at school, he and the other students were required to communicate with each other solely through speech and speechreading. Since most of the children, including John, had been through oral infant and preschool programs, upon entering the school they had enough of the rudiments of oral skills to get along.

While oral and auditory training was intensive, the school also followed a rigorous academic curriculum. John did well in both aspects of his schooling. Socially, too, he adjusted well, making several strong friendships that were to last into his college years. Despite their teachers' vigilance, John and his friends engaged in lots of nonverbal exchanges in addition to speaking. But by the sixth or seventh grade they had a strong grasp of language and were writing poems on their own and even experimenting with rhyme. Through it all, they never questioned the oral approach and, following their teachers' lead, felt superior to the signing deaf people they occasionally came across. At best the oral students felt sorry for manualists; at worst they ridiculed and looked down on them.

John did well in the public high school he entered in the ninth grade. He was confident in his speech and not above asking for special consideration—seats in the front row so he could read the teacher's speech, for example. His family was very supportive both in giving him what he needed to fit in socially, such as a car and nice clothes, and in helping him with his schoolwork. Very often he missed information in class, but his brother and sisters helped him there, and by the end of his first year he had made good friends who were always willing to share their class notes and fill in the gaps. He found the schoolwork at the public school much less demanding than that at the private oral school, and he sailed through his four years there with few problems that couldn't be solved.

In his senior year, John and his parents visited Gallaudet College, the liberal arts college for the deaf in Washington, D.C. John knew he would have to overcome his built-in bias against sign language to go to Gallaudet, since most students there were manualists or trained in total communication. Instruction was spoken and signed and the considerable social life at the college was mostly based on sign language. But his visit disappointed him. He found the academic level of the classes to be lower in some departments than in his high school classes. To him the reading requirements in most Gallaudet classes appeared to be scaled down in deference to the difficulty deaf people commonly have with reading. John decided to go to a hearing college where he would meet the same academic challenges a hearing person would face.

He decided on Beloit College, in Wisconsin, which had an active work-study program: he would work at a job for one quarter out of each year in the four-year program. At Beloit, for the first time John felt intensely the limitations of his oral skills. Most of the classes were conducted as seminars, and John had trouble following group discussions. Basically the problem lay in determining where to look first—who was speaking? who would speak next? It was a far cry from sitting in the front row in a high school class reading the speech of the teacher and filling in the gaps later with friends' class notes. The competition for grades was intense at Beloit, and the kind of socializing John was used to was at a minimum. In his first year, John felt more shy of people than he ever had, intimidated by his own flagging confidence as well as by the intellectual level of the conversations he observed. Furthermore, the reading assignments in his classes were long and complex. John ran across many unfamiliar words, both in reading and in class discussions. He could look up written ones in the dictionary, but spoken words often baffled him completely. How were they spelled? What were their connotations? He began to realize the importance of the role his family had played for him in his high school studies.

Still, with hard work and aggressive questioning, John did well at Beloit. He thrived in his work-study jobs, relying heavily on his oral skills in dealing with people he met on the job. And eventually he came to feel more comfortable socially as well. Exhilarated by the range of people in the college community, by his senior year he was seeking out all manner of people—radicals, conservatives, communists, socialists, athletes, hippies. The people he had known up to that time had been fairly homogeneous, and his native curiosity spurred him on to meet all types of people and find out how they thought. Again, he sharpened his oral skills in this way; in a sense it was a form of practice.

When John graduated, he went to Europe, traveling for a summer with an old friend from his oral-school days. After their holiday, both John and his friend decided to go to Gallaudet for a year of graduate work. During that time they breezed through their academic requirements, putting most of their energies into learning sign language. Following Gallaudet, John went into business with his father, becoming a well-respected executive. Mostly he relied on his oral skills for doing business, but in group meetings he usually used a simultaneous interpreter* to speed things up and to ensure against the possibility of his missing something important.

It is clear that John went far on his oral skills and that without them his experiences would have been considerably limited. The same was true for the two old friends he kept in touch with from his deaf-school days. Like John, both friends were pure oralists who learned sign language after finishing high school. And like him, both were successful in their fields—one was a dentist and one a psychotherapist. These three saw themselves as very different from the deaf people they knew who signed exclusively and who grew up signing. Socially they felt ill at ease with signers, because they considered the cultural and intellectual interests of the latter to be very limited. The three friends believed that signers didn't really understand the hearing world, wanted to remain apart from it, and saw themselves, whether they admitted it or not, as inferior to hearing people. The three were proud of their achievements as oralists and felt themselves to be more sophisticated than signers they knew. They felt they owed their understanding of the hearing world to the fact that they moved within it freely, using the same mode of communication that hearing people used.

Sandra

Sandra's story was told to us by Rose, an experienced teacher of the deaf who had switched from oralism to total commu-

---

*A simultaneous interpreter is one who interprets both sides of a conversation—signing and speaking to the deaf participant trained in total communication and speaking to the hearing participant. Thus the deaf person doesn't lose a message due to the logistics of a group discussion and the hearing person isn't hampered by an unfamiliarity with deaf speech or an ignorance of sign language.

nication after ten years of teaching. Rose told us that Sandra's story reinforced her decision to change; from it she took reassurance that she had done the right thing in switching to use of total communication in the classroom.

Sandra's parents were bent on oralism from the first. As soon as Sandra's hearing impairment was confirmed, they started the John Tracy Clinic correspondence course, a directed program for beginning oral training with preschool-age children. The no-signing role was strictly enforced at home, and at age five, Sandra was sent to a residential oral school in the next city, spending weekends and holidays with her family. She was homesick and discouraged from the start, and her loneliness was made worse by the staff's vigilance regarding sign language and gestures. Many of the smaller children, not advanced enough in their oral training to speak with each other, spent much of their free time watching television.

Sandra grew shy and proved slow to acquire speech skills. Even when she was certain she could express herself, she was usually too timid to do so. But because she wanted very much to please her parents, she continued to work diligently at speech and speechreading.

When she was seven, Sandra went to a summer camp for disabled children. There, for the first time in her life, she met a deaf child who used sign language. Secretly the two deaf girls became friends, and eventually, though signing had been strictly banned to her, Sandra allowed the other girl to teach her sign language. She picked it up quickly and was soon good enough at signing to feel she was in real communication with her friend. The girls met secretly as often as they could, but near the end of the summer a counselor caught them signing and, aware of Sandra's oral training, angrily and forcibly separated them (perhaps out of concern for her own job security). Sandra was grief stricken at the loss of her friend but also guilt ridden at having dabbled in the forbidden language of sign. She was frightened, too, by the counselor's angry manner.

Sandra stayed in the residential school throughout high school and eventually became proficient enough in speech to enroll in college. Her choice, like John's, was a small, private college. She never considered Gallaudet College; the dominance of sign language there put her off completely. Never once, after her intimidating experience at camp, did she think of sign language as anything other than degrading and taboo.

Rose, the teacher who related Sandra's story to us, had worked at Sandra's school before her conversion to a total communication philosophy. In her last year of college, Sandra visited Rose, and Rose invited her former student to observe at the school where she was teaching. Sandra was silent and noncommittal as she visited a number of classrooms but was clearly interested in all that was going on. Following the visit, the two went out to lunch, and when they were seated in the restaurant, to Rose's great surprise, Sandra began to cry.

"What is it? Have I done something wrong?" asked Rose.

After gaining control of herself, Sandra looked at her steadily and said, "I resent you so much for denying me the right to be a deaf person."

"What?" exclaimed Rose in surprise. "How on earth did I do that?"

"You never let me sign—no one did. You made me believe that signing was a weakness, dirty almost, a symbol of failure. I can understand my parents doing that because they didn't know. But you—you went to school; you learned what deafness was. Now watching you with the kids in your school, I see you signing—and the children are having such a good time there with learning. It's not the struggle it was for me. They don't feel weak, as if part of them was missing that they were trying to replace by learning to speak. You denied me the right to relax and I still don't fit in anywhere. I'm not really a hearing person. I miss a lot of what's said, I still struggle hard to understand. I'm not comfortable with hearing people because I miss so much. And now, though I'm learning to sign, I'm not comfortable with signing deaf friends because I miss a lot with them too—and because, well, we seem different from each other because I can talk. I just don't fit anywhere."

It is important to perceive the irony in this story: Sandra's ability to express her feelings so fully to a hearing person was owed completely to her oral skills. But her inner struggle and her confusion of loyalties were no less painful for all that. The questions "Where does my child belong?" and "Where do I want my child to fit in?" are fundamental to the problem of which method you will choose.

We told an oral teacher Sandra's story, and she expressed dismay at Sandra's lack of facility at signing. "Sign language is not difficult to learn later in life—Sandra will be fluent soon. Then she'll see that the delay was worthwhile, since she will have the skills to enter both worlds, not just one or the other. Had she been allowed to learn to sign earlier, she might never have gained the speech that allowed her to take Rose to task." Supporters of total communication would retort, "Yes, but what if she hadn't learned speech at all? All those years would have been wasted."

Obviously, the oral-totalist debate remains unresolved. The stories of John and Sandra are just two out of millions. Perhaps any case history would shed a new light on the problem and make the weighing of costs and benefits that much more complicated. Still, it is just this sort of personal history that is most instructive. We urge you to seek out deaf adults of both persuasions and weigh their responses to their training. Ultimately, the decision regarding sign language is a personal one. We can only hope that once you make the decision on behalf of your child, you will remain alert to your child's progress and clear-sighted enough to continually rethink the question.

EVALUATING AN ORAL PROGRAM

If you have located an oral program that seems feasible to you geographically and financially, what steps can you take to determine its educational value? Basically, you will need to assure yourself that the program is designed to teach oral skills and provide a strong academic curriculum.

To reiterate, the central belief in the oralist philosophy is that teaching speech and the comprehension of speech should be the primary object in educating the deaf. Oralists attempt to provide deaf children with the tools that will enable them to become integrated in the hearing world—speech and speech-reading. They argue that with these tools deaf people have the same opportunities as hearing people to participate in and benefit from society and that without them deaf people are cut off from most of society, psychologically if not functionally. Oralists prohibit sign language on the premise that a child using it will be too distracted by it or too attracted by its comparative ease to persevere in the colossally difficult task of learning to speak without being able to hear.

Spoken Language and Feedback

For the profoundly and severely deaf, learning to speak is something like learning to swim without ever setting foot in the water. Deaf people never have the chance to test their pronunciation; they never know when they are mispronouncing a word—or some words, or *all* words—without being told. Often, when they are unable to make themselves understood, deaf speakers are not sure why and have no clues on how they can improve their speech. Teachers in an oral-school program must provide the feedback that hearing people receive automatically whenever they enter a conversation. Thus, the first component of a good oral program must be intensive and supportive speech training.

Speechreading

The other half of an oral program is teaching children to speak through speechreading. This, the receptive component of the oral method, is no less difficult and fraught with imprecision. Estimates of the amount of spoken language that is incomprehensible through speechreading alone range from 50 to 80 percent, varying from person to person. Too many sounds resemble others on the lips for any more accuracy to be guaranteed, except for a very small group who are the most proficient speechreaders. With this fact in mind, imagine the difficulty of young children just learning to discriminate among minute lip, tongue, and facial movements. The task strains the attention of the most experienced adult speech-reader.

Nevertheless, it can be done: Children do learn to comprehend the speech of hearing people and other deaf oralists. They use a combination of speechreading and high-level guess-work based on a familiarity with the language. And young children do learn to speak, with varying degrees of intelligibility. Some oralists are such successful speakers and make such excellent use of their residual hearing (see the next section) that they are able to use the telephone. The only limit on the ability of many "oral successes" to communicate with anyone, hearing or deaf, is their proficiency in the language itself. A strong oral program, then, is also a strong language program. (We return to this complex point in a later section and again in Chapter 5.)

Auditory Training

In recent decades, the completeness of the silence that deaf people, even profoundly deaf people, experience has been called into question by advances in audiological assessments and amplification. It is now believed that most deaf people have some residual hearing and that amplification can have beneficial effects on people whose deafness would have been considered total in the recent past. Even where there is no certainty that amplification will help, using it is worth the trouble and expense, since assessing accurately the level of deafness in babies and young children is impossible (see page 106). Thus, the best oral programs are in effect no longer purely oral but have become aural-oral, or oral-auditory, by making the fullest use of hearing aids and classroom amplification systems.

This new emphasis on amplification incidentally provides parents with one means of assessing an oral program. Does the school use amplification fully? Do the teachers check hearing aids thoroughly and throughout the day, or are hearing-aid checks, when they are done at all, superficial and therefore all but useless? Do the teachers *really* know when children are not receiving all the sounds they could through hearing aids?

Also, in assessing an oral program you should assure yourself that your child's auditory education will include training in *using* sounds: discriminating among them, determining where they come from and how they relate to speech. Without such training, deaf children are unable to make sense of the sounds they do hear. With good auditory training, they are sometimes able to gain more from their amplified hearing than anyone judging solely from their audiograms could have predicted or hoped. In this regard, a parent might make a point of determining how lessons are presented to reinforce the development of listening skills. Are all sounds presented in full view of the children? Or are the children challenged auditorally to use their residual hearing?

Learning Language

As a group, deaf people have always had poor reading skills, and the situation has not improved over time. Most deaf high school graduates read at a fourth-grade level, even today. Parents need to assure themselves that the oral program they are considering addresses the reading problem aggressively.

To make sure you understand why deaf children can have trouble learning to read, we must return once more to our definitions:

> *language* is a symbolic system for communicating ideas and feelings;
> *speech* is audible language created by the mouth, tongue, voice box, and breath.

Speech is a vehicle for language; signs are another, and writing is another.

A child who learns speech by imitation, which, in its very simplest interpretation, is how oralism works, does not automatically learn language. Have you ever learned the lyrics to a song in a foreign language that you didn't understand? Your lack of comprehension did not necessarily affect how well you sang the song, especially if you are a good imitator and had a good model (someone who sang the song clearly and whom you could copy). The principle is the same: Deaf children can learn to imitate speech to some extent without necessarily understanding the language. However, it is impossible to speechread without understanding the language—English, in our case—since the guesswork required depends on a knowledge both of vocabulary and grammar. Language acquisition involves (1) learning words' meanings and (2) learning the accepted means of putting words together to make messages that others who use the language will understand. Imitating language, then, is a separate activity from learning to speak.

In earlier chapters we emphasized the importance of immersing your child in communication from the very start. Speechreading skills can start to grow from infancy onward, and oral infant-programs exist to encourage the growth of these skills and guide parents in encouraging them. Directed speechreading exercises plus a home environment in which communication flows freely can begin to introduce a deaf child to the complicated tool we call language (see Chapter 5 for ways of making language accessible to your child at home).

Parents can learn which words to use, which sounds are most visible, which are most audible, and how to speak to the child learning oral language skills. But parents should not take on full responsibility for teaching their children language. Every language is a complex system, and teaching language, both to hearing and deaf people, is a highly developed technical skill. Your responsibility as a parent lies not in teaching but in making sure that the school you choose conveys a solid understanding of language and its relationship to speech.

You should know that some purely auditory programs (programs that focus on residual hearing alone, training deaf children to develop their listening skills) as well as some oral programs delay instruction in reading and writing in order to emphasize the development of speech and listening skills. The rationale is that learning oral skills is so important for young children that other subjects become secondary for a while. With this situation in mind, vigilant parents must ascertain that their school program is providing adequate language—as well as speech—training.

Children not properly exposed to language from an early age often fail not only to read and write well but also to speak and understand, which are the main objectives of oral training. Like children who are taught the rudiments of swimming but are kept from the water for years, these "oral failures," as they are called, do not understand the medium and never gain control of it. But whereas swimmers can learn, eventually, the qualities and potential power of water, the medium of language is so vastly complex and composed of so many parts and rules that children not immersed in it early often lose heart. And if not encouraged, they can remain perpetually bewildered. Remember: Every word deaf children learn—until they know language well enough to use a dictionary—they must be taught. The same holds true for every rule, every technique for changing forms of words, every tense, every mood—every one of a thousand details that give hearing children headaches in grammar lessons. Somehow these details must all be made clear to deaf children, starting at the beginning of their education.

To summarize, word pronunciation, though itself a daily challenge for a deaf child, is only one aspect of oral communication. The even more taxing aspects relate to understanding language. And learning to read and write is totally dependent on language comprehension. In assessing an oral program, you must assure yourself that the teachers teach language as well as speech. Otherwise, your child could be imitating a series of sounds without being able to form intelligible messages. An equally serious risk is that the child will fail to feel at ease with the written word. To a deaf person, the ability to read means independence, the freedom to gather information at will, without having to rely on others for instruction. No matter what program we choose, then, we must make sure our deaf children learn to read and write.

Academic Subjects

On one level you must evaluate an oral program as you would any school program. Thus, as evaluator you must ask, What about history, English, mathematics, science, and art in the oral program you are considering? Will the school provide its students with a good education in addition to stressing the oral skills? After all, your concern is for your whole child, not just his or her eyes, ears, or mouth. It is the hearing, not the need to know, that is impaired. As in the home environment, the goal is to provide the best possible school environment for children who happen to be deaf, not for deaf children whose chief characteristic is their hearing impairment.

ORALISM: WHAT OBSERVERS SAY

What follows is an overview of reactions to oralism by deaf people and professionals in the field of deafness. We present a range of comments, from endorsement to criticism, because the research on the effects of oral training is inconclusive. To evaluate oralism, we must collect the full range of opinions and test them against our own inclinations and experience.

It is important to state that *everyone,* oralism's critics and supporters alike, acknowledges the importance of speech and language skills. To have no speech and poor language is to be completely cut off from the mainstream of society. But, again, the question is not whether deaf children should be taught oral skills but whether they should be taught oral skills *exclusively.* The following sections survey several characteristic results of strict oralist training.

Those Who Won't Use Their Oral Skills

Reactions to oralism from deaf people who have been through oral training range from love to hate for the philosophy. On the hate side are those who recall hour after hour, day after day, and year after year of speech and speechreading training—often with results not satisfying enough to justify the time and energy spent. Many orally trained deaf people, though successful by the standards of their school programs, are self-conscious about using their speech with hearing people. They know they have "deaf speech" and that hearing people often have trouble understanding them.

Those Who Do

On the other side are the living examples of the oralist's dream: deaf people who use their speech skills freely in the hearing world and who, because of their ability to communicate with hearing people, do not suffer from the sense of inferiority that many nonverbal deaf people feel. Such oralists are often notably successful in their professions. In fact, although no census confirms the link, high ambition and professional success among deaf people have traditionally been associated with oral training. Whether oralism leads to success or whether only the most ambitious and success-oriented deaf people learn oral skills remains to be determined. Furthermore, whether the association between oralism and professional success will continue to hold true as more and more graduates of total communication programs enter professional life is as yet unknown.

The significant factor in oral success might be a kind of personal and social adjustment altogether unrelated to speech skills. A child who feels accepted as a person and at ease in the world, whose self-esteem and self-acceptance are not put at risk by moments of bewilderment or social awkwardness, will be more willing to take a chance at mispronouncing a word or being misunderstood than a child on the brink of self-contempt. As we have said, the crucial difference for deaf children lies in the home environment. Children shut out from family life because they are deaf can come to believe that they simply have nothing to say. If such a child does manage to acquire oral skills, he or she might be understandably reluctant to use them.

Those Who Can't

Critics of oralism point to another sort of oral "result" as demonstrating the real risk of oralism. This is the group of graduates or dropouts—admittedly large though so far unmeasured—who in spite of years of oral training have failed to acquire speech skills. Because of oralism's prohibition against sign language, it is conceivable for such "oral failures" to go through most of their school years and sometimes most or all of their lives without a means of communicating with others, though in practice they usually begin to learn sign language after leaving their oral programs (as do many successful oralists, for social purposes).

In making a commitment to an oral program, you *must* know that it is possible for your child to fail to learn oral skills. Even when optimum conditions for oral training have been met—infant programs, strong auditory and language training, excellent teachers and facilities—many children in oral programs never learn to speak and speechread well enough to communicate effectively. It is easy, and probably natural, when your child is doing poorly, to deceive yourself into thinking, "Perhaps she just needs one more year. One more year at school and she will begin to talk and speechread." But if the child simply cannot learn to speak and to read speech, one last year might delay just that much longer the child's chances to gain another means of communication.

As we indicated in Chapter 1, the ability to rid oneself of self-deception and to accept the limitations of a situation is perhaps the greatest challenge facing the parent of a hearing-impaired child. But without such acceptance parents will be unable to perform their crucial role as monitors of their children's education.

In your attempts to view your child's progress realistically, unclouded by wishful thinking, it should help you to realize that a deaf person's facility in oral skills is not a reflection of intelligence. It is more accurate to think of oral facility, both expressive and receptive, as a talent, similar to that for playing the piano. Some deeply insightful deaf people have no flair for oral skills at all, while some with only a superficial understanding of the world are impressive speakers and speechreaders. The difficulty lies with the fact that, as with those who want to play the piano, there is no way of telling beforehand who will succeed and who will fail, no matter how many hours a day they practice. Some oralists suggest that children who have potential for oral success can be identified through attention to five factors: (1) age at onset of hearing loss; (2) cause of hearing loss; (3) pattern of the loss (that is, the range of sounds affected); (4) age at which the child is fitted with an appropriate hearing aid; and (5) extent of the family's support. To date, however, no means of predicting success has proved reliable. It is for this reason that close monitoring is crucial.

To summarize, if you decide on an oral program, you must prime yourself to determine whether or not your child actually makes progress in acquiring oral skills. Simultaneously, your attention to the child's self-image and participation in communication at home will go far toward enabling him or her actually to use the speech and speechreading acquired.

TOTAL COMMUNICATION

The term *total communication (TC)* covers a wide range of educational methods. In its strictest use the term means communication through oral skills, sign language, auditory training, and visual aids. On the other end of the spectrum more liberal "totalists" use the term to encompass oral skills, sign language, *plus* anything and everything—gestures, mime, note writing, standing on the head—that succeeds in getting messages across from hearing to deaf people and from deaf to hearing. But the distinguishing feature shared by every total communication program is the *combination* of the tools of communication. In practice this means that every message conveyed in the classroom is made unambiguous for the deaf child by whatever means are required.

Totalists argue that their way has two major advantages

over oralism. First, by teaching both speech and sign language right from the start, a TC program can begin to convey information to children more quickly and enable children to communicate earlier than an oral program can. The reason is that sign language is much easier to learn than speech, especially during the early, language-acquiring years. The second benefit is a negative one: Totalists argue that total communication ensures against failure. Even if a child fails to pick up enough oral skills to interact freely in the hearing world, that child will still have a language—a sign language—and thus the means to interact, though only with the minority of others who know the language too. Total communication, the argument goes, guards against the awful possibility that children might emerge from a program as bewildered and isolated as when they entered it.

The argument is a convincing one, but as with oralism the proof is in the practice: Do TC programs really deliver on their commitment to equip deaf children with oral, signing, and language skills? Again, your role as a parent considering a total communication program is first that of evaluator and then of monitor.

Parent Participation

To participate fully in the child's total communication education and to use at home the modes of communication used at school, at least the parents—and ideally the whole household—must learn sign language. All the TC teachers we interviewed stressed the importance of parents using sign language and speech together in the home.* Where parents fail to learn sign language, whatever communication takes place at

---

*In an oral program, of course, the problem does not exist, since the mode of communication is already the same as that used at school—oral. Parents of oral students need to learn about the sounds of their language and the visibility of those sounds, but they do not have to learn a new language.

home is restricted to body language, writing, and the oral mode. Since totalists believe that sign language serves as the deaf child's bridge into the oral world, to them speaking alone is not enough. Parents of children in TC programs who don't learn sign language fail to equip themselves with the means to communicate fully with their children.

However, though learning sign language is easier than learning speech, typically parents fail to keep pace as their children become more fluent. Deaf children in TC infant, preschool, and primary-school programs are immersed in sign language from the beginning of their education, but hearing parents and siblings must make a special effort to go to classes, find time to practice, and, as they gain proficiency, enroll in more advanced classes, just as they would for any language training.

Thus, before you even visit a TC classroom to observe, you are faced with deciding whether or not you have the time and energy to learn sign language. And even if you decide to take classes, your fluency isn't guaranteed. Surveys of parents' signing abilities in the past have shown very disappointing results. Even parents who start off enthusiastically often become discouraged and stop practicing as their children's signing facility increases. The problem is compounded by the fact that one sign language plus several manual codes for English exist in the United States. This fact is the source of a new and growing controversy (covered on pages 109–118).

Some teachers who view parent involvement as absolutely necessary to a deaf child's success argue that a parent unwilling to learn sign language has in effect opted for oralism, since communication at home will be exclusively oral. Others disagree, pointing out that many children have come through residential school programs learning to communicate regardless of the mode used at home, seeing their parents only on weekends and vacations anyway. Thus, even on the issue of parents learning sign language there are no trends confirmed by research. In deciding how to proceed in this matter, once more you are basically on your own.

What's Really Going on at School?

When you decide on a TC program for your child, remember: You are opting for oralism *plus* manualism *plus* all other communicative tools, not instruction in sign language alone. Your child should receive strong auditory, speech, speechreading, language, and reading and writing training as well as instruction in sign language and a comprehensive exposure to the conventional academic curriculum. The TC teacher of the deaf simultaneously signs and speaks every message; presumably the children are taught to do the same. Thus, they are developing two modes of communication at once—in the long view, gaining access to both the hearing and the deaf worlds.

But what *really* goes on in a given TC program at any particular time? This comprehensive approach is a tall order. Your role as a concerned observer is to see that it is being filled. The first question to ask is whether oral skills are truly being stressed or whether the teacher is relying on sign language alone as the primary mode of communication. And again, is the auditory training being carried out adequately, and are thorough hearing-aid checks completed?

Some critics go much further in analyzing the TC approach, wondering whether it is possible at all to meet the needs of a classroom of deaf children, each with a particular combination of limitations and skills. Consider, for example, just three six-year-old children who might easily wind up in the same TC classroom:

Aaron, profoundly deaf, has almost no communicative skills of any kind. He is sullen, withdrawn, restless, and inattentive.

Laurie, with strong residual hearing, has excellent oral skills but has been made self-conscious by hearing children about using her speech. She needs to be encouraged to talk and to take pride in her achievements.

Ben, whose deafness is severe, has been slow to talk and speechread and even slower to sign. His frustration at his lack of progress is getting explosive; he needs help in expressing himself in both modes, and soon, for his anger is becoming disruptive to the class and to his own learning process.

How is a teacher to meet the special needs of each of these children, and of the six or eight—or twelve or even twenty—others who might make up the class?

Basic to a good TC teacher's approach is a consistent commitment to the speaking/signing role. No matter what they do, no matter which child they are attending to at the time, such teachers speak and sign every message, thus simultaneously reinforcing manual, oral, and auditory skills. The rest is a matter of emphasis. Thus:

> For Aaron, the teacher would primarily strive to engage his interest, help him focus on these strange movements of the lips and the hands, and concentrate on his hearing as a possible source of stimulation. Or the teacher might draw him into the circle of activity by means of a rabbit or a puzzle or a book.
>
> To Laurie, the teacher would direct hard questions, helping the girl to lose her self-consciousness in the process of forming answers.
>
> For Ben, the teacher would bring to bear all the techniques of psychology and patient encouragement he or she had ever learned while helping him to become acquainted with the tools of communication as if he had never had trouble with them.

So would go this ideal teacher's dance—he or she would juggle the separate needs of each child while drawing the whole class together in a network of communication and, above all, immersing the children in *language.*

As an observer in a TC classroom, you must assure yourself that the teacher succeeds in reaching every child. Is the class too large to allow for individual attention? Or is the level of instruction geared, as it so often is in regular classrooms, to the lowest common denominator, the Aarons or the Bens, leaving the Lauries unstimulated and unable to progress? An extension of this question is the TC opponent's most serious criticism: that TC settles for less than an optimum education, equipping children to function in a highly restricted "deaf world" rather than the society at large. In fact, critics argue that TC virtually *creates* the boundaries of the deaf world by binding deaf people together through sign language. Again, to assess a particular program you will need to view it not simply as a total communication program but as an educational program per se so that you can measure the academic challenges it offers your child.

In part, total communication can be viewed as a response to what critics of oralism have seen as the weaknesses of oralism. Thus, the philosophy and practice of the TC mode is best understood in the context of oralism and its critics' contentions. If you skipped to this section to learn about total communication, we urge you to return to pages 82–91 to gain a fuller understanding of the methods controversy.

OTHER MODES

This section covers what might be termed relatively minor modes of communication, since none has achieved the large following and widespread practice of oralism and total communication. Nevertheless, the importance of these programs— the auditory method, the Rochester method, and cued speech—should not be underestimated. The auditory method has yielded impressive results with children who have the potential to learn to hear; the Rochester method has had a long history of success and, in its Russian form, has gained wide acceptance in the Soviet Union; and cued speech seems to be gaining popularity, especially since oralists are beginning to acknowledge its value with respect to their own programs. One major limitation of these programs is their relative rarity. Not only are the programs hard to come across, but also the numbers of people proficient in these modes is relatively small. But if such programs are available to you, we urge you to investigate them with the open-mindedness with which you would assess an oral or TC program. You might find that the specifications of one of these programs matches the particular needs of your child.

The Auditory Method

We have already touched on the auditory method in connection with oralism. Oral programs are currently emphasizing auditory training more heavily than in the past, but pure auditory, or unisensory, programs still exist, designed for children with enough residual hearing to make complete dependence on amplified hearing a realistic goal. Again, mistakes have been made, and children with no chance of developing adequate hearing skills have been doomed through enrollment in auditory programs to long years of failure and frustration. The course of action called for in determining a child's potential for a pure auditory program must begin, of course, with the best audiological evaluation possible. But accurately measuring a very young child's residual hearing is difficult, which means that assessing his or her potential for success in an auditory program is difficult as well. The results of an audiological test in a two- or three-year-old, say, largely depend on the child's voluntary or involuntary reactions to sounds. Who knows what the child might hear, or realize he hears, were he trained to focus attention on the test sounds? If the child has a cold or if the Eustachian tubes are clogged, the test might be affected considerably. And again, who knows what roles are played by the child's mood, the parent's anxiety, or the rapport between the child and audiologist in determining the existing hearing that actually gets measured? Thus, initial evaluation must go hand in hand with alert monitoring. Just as on the one hand appropriate amplification plus consistent auditory training might yield results far beyond the predictions of audiologists of a decade ago, so too, on the other hand, might auditory training for a child unable to hear or process sounds within the range of human speech be completely in vain, yielding nothing but disappointment and continued isolation.

The Rochester Method

The Rochester method is the simultaneous use of speech and fingerspelling, a form of sign language in which finger formations represent individual letters (used in other sign languages, too, where a name or an unfamiliar word is being signed). In theory, fingerspelling every word that is spoken provides the child with a strong language model, since the child sees every part of every word—all plurals and all endings, every article and connective, parts that can get lost in sign language or speechreading. In practice, however, fingerspelling every word can be laborious; thus, children using it tend to invent or incorporate signs and gestures from elsewhere as a shorthand. The result, from a language purist's point of view, is the contamination of English. Still, a responsible, highly committed teacher of this method presumably conveys the perfect language model to his or her students. For many people it takes considerably longer to fingerspell a message than to speak it, though the most proficient fingerspellers can communicate at the rate of speech.

A great advantage of fingerspelling, though, is that it is easy for parents and others to learn, even in a few hours. Therefore, it can serve as a guaranteed means of communication, though a slow one, where parents are unable to learn sign language or to feel satisfied communicating in a purely oral mode. The method is, of course, limited by age, since motor development in children up to about four is usually insufficient for fingerspelling. Furthermore, a fingerspeller must know how to spell and to read. A family inclined toward manualism might find itself launched in another signing system long before their child reaches the age at which these limitations can be overcome.

It is interesting to note that the Rochester method, which is currently practiced in only a few schools in the country (not necessarily a measure of its effectiveness), is similar to the method called neo-oralism adopted throughout the Soviet Union and acclaimed there for its success. The Rochester method may well have its strengths for those willing or able to commit themselves to fingerspelling consistently every word they speak.

Cued Speech

Cued speech is a method currently gaining popularity across the country, even, in some places, among oralists who would otherwise reject the use of a manual component in their mode of communication. In fact, cued speech was invented to compensate for the difficulties oralism presents and was fully intended for use by committed oralists. The method is manual in the sense that it uses hand movements in combination with speech, but in this case the hand movements represent sounds, not words, ideas, or letters. The cues inform the receiver as to which *sounds* are actually being made as the speaker speaks—information that the uncued speechreader has to guess at least 50 percent—some say 80 percent—of the time. Eight hand shapes in four positions constitute the complete system of manual cues; thus, the whole system can be comprehended quickly, though becoming proficient takes much time and practice. A further advantage is that whereas sign languages have to be adapted or "translated" (a complex topic covered in the next section), cues apply to English as it is spoken. Thus, the child learns English purely, as it is used in the hearing world.

The difficulty with cued speech, critics say, is that to use it one must think phonetically—that is, to break down words into their component sounds, not, as is easier for speakers who also write their language, into syllables as written. Critics claim that few parents could develop the proficiency in thinking phonetically that they would need for cuing everything they said—for example, instantaneously realizing that *phone* began with *f,* not *p.* Many teachers have difficulty doing this, so expecting parents to learn to cue at a normal speech rate may be asking a lot.

A further difficulty is teaching deaf children themselves to cue accurately in transmitting their own messages. How do you teach a child to recognize and represent sounds manually when he or she has never heard them?

Finally, cued speech suffers the disadvantage of any of the "minor" modes: So few people know and practice cuing that a child dependent on the system would be unlikely to find other users in society at large.

Still, cued speech does enable children to learn English, and those who learn English can learn to read without having to learn a new language first, which, as the following section will show, many signers must do. The same is true of the Rochester method. This feature itself weighs heavily in the methods controversy, since the importance of reading is acknowledged by everyone. For deaf even more than hearing children, reading offers a way of filling in the inevitable gaps, of pursuing information or pleasure independently, and of exploring the language without thinking about how it sounds.

THE "NEW" CONTROVERSY: ASL VERSUS ENGLISH

Were the oral-manual controversy resolved tomorrow, the methods debate would still be far from over. In total communication circles particularly, a new argument is surfacing that divides educators who might otherwise feel unified by the total communication approach. Once more, sign language is at issue, but this time instead of "Should sign language be used in school?" the question is *"Which language* should be emphasized during a total communication program and at which points?"

"Which language?" you might cry, bewildered. "But how many languages are there?"

The answer is that when it comes to manual communication there are *two* languages in the United States: English and American Sign Language (ASL). English, as everyone knows, is the native language of most United States citizens. ASL, as relatively few hearing people know, is the native language of some American deaf people

Readers who have until now been unaware of the existence

of American Sign Language will doubtless have many questions: Where did it come from? What is it like? How is it passed on? But for the moment, let's concentrate not on the origins or qualities of ASL but simply on its existence as one of two languages available for manual communication. We'll approach this complex subject one step at a time and hope that all questions will eventually be answered in the course of the discussion.

ASL is a manual-visible language—it was never anything other than a sign language. English, however, is primarily a spoken language. In order for English to be used as a sign language it must be represented by a *manual code,* a system of signs that make it visible. Other examples of codes are Braille, which makes English tangible, Morse code, which makes it transmittable electronically, and semaphore. The latter, like manual codes, makes English visible, but through flags rather than manual signs.

For manual communication in the United States the two languages occupy opposite ends of a spectrum:

ASL◄————————————————►English

A number of different manual codes exist for communicating in English, however. Thus, there is *only one sign language* (ASL), but there are a number of manual codes, or systems for making English visible manually:

ASL◄————————————► English
                                  1. Fingerspelling
                                  2. Cued Speech
                                  3. Seeing Essential English (SEE I)
                                  4. Signing Exact English (SEE II)
                                  5. Linguistics of Visual English (LOVE)

We say that ASL and English exist on a spectrum because a manual communication exchange can be characterized by *more* or *less* ASL depending on the circumstances and on the fluency of the participants in ASL or English. Manual-communication exchanges can be conducted purely in ASL, purely in English, or in a blend of ASL and English with varying proportions of both languages depending on the knowledge of the participants. No strict boundaries exist among these various types of exchanges. However, the blended version, which uses elements of both languages in varying degrees, is called Pidgin Sign English (PSE). Thus, the manual-communication continuum in the United States looks like this:

ASL◄─────────────────────►English
Pidgin Sign English (PSE)

People move along the continuum between the two extremes depending on two factors. The first is how much ASL and English the participants know. The more ASL the English-speaking participant knows, the more the pidgin form used resembles ASL; the less ASL the English speaker knows, the more the pidgin form used resembles English. Much manual communication is conducted in this fluid pidgin language, which incorporates elements from the native languages of both the deaf and hearing worlds. If you take a sign language course that, like most beginning courses, teaches you little more than vocabulary, you and your child will devise your own version of Pidgin Sign English. You will see for yourself not only how effective this combined form can be but also how responsive it is to improvements in your proficiency.

The second factor affecting the degree of ASL in a PSE exchange is the social circumstances under which the exchange takes place. American Sign Language is a cultural phenomenon. It both binds speakers together in a community, enforcing a group identity, and keeps nonusers out. Most ASL users who are also fluent in English shift toward the English end of the spectrum when communicating with hearing people, partly to enable the exchange to take place, since until recently few hearing people had the opportunity to learn ASL. A good analogy here is that between ASL and Black English. As the language of the black subculture in America, Black English might be considered to be the real language of the black community. But black people fluent in this language shift to more standard English when conversing with white people, not only to make themselves understood but also to keep their language separate from the majority culture. In much the same way, an ASL user moves toward English when conversing with a hearing person.

American Sign Language

Let's return now to some of those original questions. What is meant by the native language of the deaf? Who speaks it? Where did this language come from? And how, you might ask, could it thrive in our midst without our knowing about it?

The origins of ASL are currently under study, since the language only recently was deemed "real" enough to be analyzed and charted by linguists. We know that American Sign Language shares some characteristics with French Sign Language, a phenomenon that can be explained historically, but its specifically American roots remain obscure. As to how ASL survived and thrived over the last century, we can assume that the main conduits from one generation to the next have been the children of deaf parents. We can guess that since ASL originated deaf parents have used it with their children (deaf and hearing) from their birth and that these children, native users, taught the deaf children they met outside their homes, in schools and social situations.

However, though ASL has been developed, refined, and kept alive by deaf people—which is why it is known as the native language of the deaf—it is not true that all deaf people learn it. For years, ASL was considered a nonlanguage, too "primitive" and "simple" to be significant, and educators did their best to keep it out of the classroom, using a wide variety of English codes and pidgin English (until the 1970s, when SEE I, SEE II, and LOVE were developed and were widely adopted as the chief English codes). And children raised as oralists, of course, were not allowed to sign at all; therefore, they were rarely exposed to ASL in their early years. Thus, many deaf signers learned to sign manually coded English only; others learned ASL, but late in their lives. Many others, however, learned *only* ASL, and still others, those with the most varied exposure, learned both English and ASL. Therefore, though theoretically ASL as a native language binds deaf people together and contributes to a sense of community, deaf people are divided by their level of fluency in each of the languages of manual communication—ASL and English.

ASL and English: How They Differ

ASL—or Ameslan, as it is also called—has its own vocabulary, its own grammar, its own word order, and its own history. In none of its elements is ASL even remotely similar to English. Most hearing people mistakenly assume that a sign-language conversation they observe between two deaf people is nothing more than a translation of an English conversation. When the language being signed is English, this assumption is true. But such a conversation, especially if it is a purely social one, is very likely to be conducted in ASL. Without proper instruction in word order and grammar, observers knowing the meaning of signs alone would have to use guesswork to understand, much as they would if they had memorized, say, a substantial vocabulary list in Russian and tried to follow a discussion in that language.

Manually coded English, on the other hand, reflects English, particularly English word order, precisely. Furthermore, it contains signs for certain parts of words known as grammatical markers—for example, "ing" and "ed"—which make verb forms in the sign language correspond to those used in English to express tense and condition. ASL has no signs per se for these markers. Rather, it uses certain specific facial expressions or body movements—as opposed to manual signs—to convey what "ed" or "ing" convey in English.

Facial expression and body language also play an important role in carrying the meaning of modifiers. For example, to express "I walk carefully," the signer in ASL would sign "I" and "walk" only, using a certain specific facial expression—a particular lip shape—to convey "carefully." Varying the lip movements would alter the meaning to "warily" or "clumsily," for instance. For years, the significance of these subtle but meaningful facial and body movements escaped non-ASL-using observers, which accounts in part for the fact that ASL was considered too simplistic to warrant study as a language. These observers were missing a significant portion of the messages by failing to recognize various movements and expressions as meaningful parts of the language.

Many native ASL users consider manually coded English too superficial to be adequately expressive. The manual codes use one sign per word, rather than modulating and shaping messages with facial expressions and gestures—all parts of ASL itself and all having a wider range of expressiveness than the codes' signs. In fact, many native ASL users have difficulty determining when an English signer is being humorous or sarcastic, for example. ASL users depend on facial expression and body language to replace voice intonation, which for a hearing person carries the tone and much of the meaning of a spoken message. All in all, native ASL users generally believe that the manual English codes are incapable of ASL's subtlety.

Another objection is that the English codes are imprecise. For example, for simplicity's sake, one code uses a single sign to symbolize all meanings of a particular word. Thus, in the following sentences the word *run* would be conveyed by the same sign despite the differences in meaning:

> I run a fever.
> I run a business.
> I run to work.
> I have a run in my stocking.

In ASL, each of the meanings of *run* shown here is conveyed by a different sign. Native signers consider that the precision gained through such separate signs enriches their language as compared with the manual codes.

Another distinction between ASL and manually coded English—that involving word order—has important ramifications for the classroom controversy. In English, word order is an important factor in the meaning of a message. Often, changing the word order of a sentence or phrase changes the meaning. In ASL, however, word order is flexible; that is, altering word order does not necessarily affect the meaning of a sentence. For this reason, and because of the other distinctions cited above, the structure of messages in ASL and English rarely correspond. This point will have significance in the next section, where we consider the relevance of the manual-communication spectrum for the classroom.

The Question in the Schools
What significance does the manual-communication continuum have for the education of your child? In the best of circumstances at a total communication school, it could mean that the child has a chance to become fluent in two languages, ASL and English, and literate in English (since ASL is not a written language). In the worst, it could spell confusion and inconsistency in the child's education.

Disagreements surround the question of which language should be taught and used at which points in school. Until recently, as noted earlier, ASL was considered by hearing people, and particularly hearing educators of the deaf, to be an inferior language, too primitive to be taken seriously. But now, since ASL has gained the attention of linguists and acknowledgment as a bona fide language, a movement has grown up to bring it into the schools. Much of the support for this movement has come from the deaf community itself. "What's wrong with our own language?" ask proponents of ASL. "Why treat it as if it weren't good enough for teaching our children? After all, we already know it." Those who hold this view do not deny the importance of teaching English, but rather intend for ASL to be used as a *bridge* to English, much as Spanish would be used to teach English to a class of native Spanish-speakers.

Proponents of manually coded English, on the other hand, argue for keeping ASL out of the classroom altogether. They believe that the relative lack of success in teaching deaf children English in the past has been due to a failure of school programs to immerse children in English. To date, those educators favoring English exclusively are in the majority across the country.

Generally, however, native users of ASL consider manually coded English to be artificial, restrictive, and inadequate as a means of self-expression. One teacher of deaf junior high school students explained that, though ASL was banned in her school, she found it necessary to shift into it (though she wasn't very fluent) when the discussion began to get conceptual or emotional. She would present the lesson in English—signing and speaking, since the program was a total communication one—and break into ASL for the class discussion. Thus, she might lecture in English on the history of capital punishment but lead a heated class discussion on the pros and cons in ASL. "We would never talk for long about the issues that hit home," she told us, "without shifting into ASL. And we couldn't talk about boys, girls, sex, parents, home life, sports, or deafness—the things that really matter to junior high kids—without it." She also reported that in working with younger children she often read and signed a story in English, then shifted to ASL to explain details and involve the children in a discussion of the story.

This teacher's experiences in support of using ASL in the classroom also inadvertently reflect two reasons for keeping it out. The first is that in a true total communication setting, where every message is signed and spoken simultaneously, ASL is impossible to use with spoken English, since the two languages are completely different. Above all, word order in

English is strictly determined, while in ASL word order is flexible. Thus, a sentence spoken in English and signed in ASL would not correspond at all.

The second difficulty is that until recently few teachers have had the opportunity to learn ASL. As noted earlier, a native language has the effect not only of binding speakers together into a community but also of keeping nonusers out. Most ASL users communicating with hearing people shift toward the English end of the spectrum to make a signed conversation possible. And the hearing world's lack of acknowledgment of ASL's validity until recently—not to mention the general ignorance of its existence—made it difficult for English speakers even to witness ASL being used, let alone to learn it.

Things are changing now. The first textbooks for teaching ASL to teachers are appearing, and classes in ASL are showing up in curricula for teachers of the deaf. A new appreciation is growing among educators of the deaf for the rich expressiveness of ASL, and some are coming to see ASL as a possible boost to deaf children's self-esteem in its potential to link them to the deaf community. But as ASL supporters gain strength, the opposing side, composed of those supporting signed English as the means of grounding deaf children in English, also gathers power. The debate is growing hotter, and resolution of the problem could be years away.

For parents of deaf children, the conflict poses difficult practical problems. But once again we can only present the options, leaving you to draw your own conclusions. In this case, the options regarding sign language use in total communication programs are these:

1. Teach ASL alone, eliminating speech in favor of good manual communication (this option is generally favored most by deaf parents of deaf children).
2. Teach ASL first to serve as a bridge to English and speech.
3. Teach English and speech only.
4. Teach English and speech, *plus* ASL as a separate language.

A second problem arises from the existing array of manual codes for English. Schools with total communication programs do not always have a clear policy regarding which manual code is to be used in a classroom. Thus, a number of teachers in the same program might use different systems. Under such circumstances, it would not be impossible for children to pass unprepared from one code to another as they pass from one classroom or grade level to another. Such inconsistency could shatter not only the progress the child made in the preceding year but the child's self-confidence as well. From your point of view, the first step toward ensuring consistency regarding sign language in the classroom is to familiarize yourself with the existing codes and to arm yourself with the right questions for assessing programs. We hope that this section has given you the tools you need to do so.

Chapter 5

Reading the World

WE BEGIN THIS CHAPTER with a warning that should serve simultaneously as a reassurance. The chapter as a whole is on language and deafness—a complex subject bordering on the technical. With this in mind, be warned: It is not your role as a parent to function as a teacher in the home. You cannot expect of yourself that, untrained and unguided, you will be able to instruct your child in language and be responsible for his or her progress. Nevertheless, by understanding the special problems in language learning your child faces and by providing an environment where language is made accessible, you can contribute greatly to his or her education. You will find this warning repeated throughout the chapter to underscore its importance for your own well-being and sense of proportion.

In this chapter it is necessary to focus on and accept a most disturbing fact, touched on briefly in the last chapter. Despite all the efforts of educators over the past hundred years, the average reading level of deaf people in the United States has remained seriously low. At present, for deaf high school graduates the average reading level measures between the fourth- and fifth-grade level. For deaf college students, the average reading level is the tenth-grade level.

As suggested earlier, deaf people have perhaps an even greater need to read than hearing people, since their means of acquiring information are limited by their hearing impairments. Therefore, the statistics on literacy reflect a serious secondary handicap—poor reading skills—among people who already face serious communication problems due to their deafness.

But the explanation for the relatively poor reading skills among deaf people hinges on an even more serious problem: Deaf people who read poorly generally have a weak grasp of the language being read. This means that deaf people who have trouble reading in English may well have difficulty both understanding others and expressing themselves in any form of the language, be it written, spoken, or signed through the use of manual codes.

Unfortunately for deaf people plagued by substandard language skills, this problem remains relatively unknown to hearing people. Many parents and, sadly, many teachers of the deaf mistakenly assume that if a deaf person can communicate on any level, either through speech or sign language, then that person knows language well enough to learn in precisely the same way and at the same rate as hearing people of the same age. Among parents this misconception is often reflected in the mistaken belief that once the child learns a mode of communication the difference between the deaf child and hearing peers will be basically evened out. Among teachers the misconception reflects an equally dangerous notion: "Well, I know how to teach, and I can communicate with deaf children—via sign language or speech. Thus, to teach deaf children effectively all I need to do is to combine the two skills." In reality, the delay that most prelingually deaf children experience before they begin to pick up language affects their learning patterns at least throughout their school years. Since language is the vehicle by which we transmit information—whether in speech, sign language, fingerspelling, or written words—a lag in language acquisition will be felt in all other areas of learning.

Before discussing in detail why prelingually deaf people have difficulties with language learning, let's distinguish once more among those old, familiar terms: *communication, language, speech, signing,* and *writing.* Very basically, *communication* is interaction that conveys information among any living creatures. *Language* is the principal tool human beings use for communicating. *Speech, signing,* and *written language* are various forms of language. To use a crude image, if language were an apple, speech, signing, and written language might be a sliced apple, a diced apple, and a bowl of apple sauce—that is, different forms of the same thing. A deaf person who hasn't managed to take in the apple sauce, written language, very often has failed to eat the apple in any of its forms.

But why is language learning difficult for the prelingually deaf?

Think about our language, English. Marvel at its complexity. Consider your own familiarity with English and how you came to feel comfortable with it. How is it that in a conversation with a friend you can manipulate so easily this complicated tool, composed of thousands of interconnected bits that work smoothly only when assembled according to a long list of rules and an equally long list of exceptions?

Now think about when you learned language. If you are an average person, you began to understand language in your first year, began to speak it in your second year, and by the time you were four years old had learned almost all the fundamental rules you will ever know about understanding and expressing yourself in English.

Thus, most people gain a grasp of their native language not in the sixth, eighth, or twelfth grade, nodding over grammar lessons and writing compositions, but rather before they are four years old.

Psychologists and most lay people used to believe that children achieved this amazing verbal ability by imitating their parents. The belief was that by saying "dada" endlessly to an infant we could teach the child to imitate the sounds, and once the child had mastered that word, we would introduce a string of words of growing complexity. Now, however, it is generally accepted that children learn language not merely by imitating others or by memorizing words, but by interacting creatively with the language that is always around them. Hearing children live in a sea of language, which enters their brains via their ears. So natural to them is this ever-present verbal environment that, like fish in water, they are nearly unconscious of the fact that they live within it and absorb it gradually. But they do—they absorb language, use it, have insights about it, and gain an ease and facility with it, all with very little effort. A three-year-old's incredible ability to form a perfectly original but appropriate sentence seems to come about automatically to most hearing children everywhere, regardless of the language being learned.

But this sea of language—the invisible environment in which every hearing child grows up—does not reach deaf children through their ears, at least not fully. We assume, or hope, that some parts of language do reach deaf children auditorally via their residual hearing. In the case of many deaf children, language does not reach them at all until they are past the age when language learning would have come to them most naturally. The fact that deaf children are more or less cut off from the verbal environment, sometimes for years, is the essence of the handicaps that stem from deafness.

SHOWING CHILDREN LANGUAGE

Despite their hearing impairment, deaf children are as capable of learning language as hearing children, and many of them do learn it. Some deaf children excel in learning language, ultimately coming to feel perfectly at ease with it and in it, comprehending others and expressing themselves with no impediment whatever. The statistics on reading cited earlier, like all statistics, reflect an average only. Furthermore, they indicate only what is true now, not what can be expected or what is possible.

The fact is, deaf children can absorb the sea of language that is the natural environment of hearing children from birth. The difference is that deaf children must do it visually rather than auditorally, through their eyes rather than their ears.

For some parents, and some teachers, too, the concept of *making language visible* is a difficult one to grasp. Most hearing people associate language learning with speech. Speech is the mode through which hearing children learn language. Most hearing children acquire and perfect their language during the first years of life by speaking and listening to spoken language. For them, the other forms of language they usually learn, reading and writing, are introduced later, once the children have learned language per se by means of speech.

For deaf children, on the other hand, even the slightest delay in introducing the visible forms of language—written language, signing, or speechreading—is a waste of precious time. Language can *only* be made available to these children through their eyes. Very specifically, then, what we mean by *making language visible* to deaf children is this: Where you would use the spoken word with a hearing baby, present a *visible* form of that word to the deaf child—write the word and sign it or speak it to the eyes, according to the mode of communication you have settled on.

Many parents balk at the notion of "forcing" written language on children of two and three years old. But once we accept the basic fact that deaf children receive all their information about language through their eyes, written language takes on a new significance. We usually allow hearing children to develop a firm grounding in language based on what they learn auditorally before we begin teaching them to read and write. But for deaf children, writing has the same significance as any other visual cue. A written word could have exactly the same impact as a sign or a word read from the lips—and all three, with repetition in the right context, can result in the child's understanding the connections among the written word and the sign or spoken word and the thing they symbolize. Even before a child knows the alphabet or knows how written language can be used, he or she can learn to recognize written words. Sensitive parents and teachers intent on exposing hearing-impaired children to language from a very early age should be prepared to make full use of written language long before they would do so with hearing children.

There is a subtle difference between starting to make language available to the child visually and actually teaching him or her how to read. Perhaps the difference lies in the intent of the teachers and parents rather than in the actual practice. Where very young children are concerned, the intention is not to set them to reading books by age three but to make them aware of the language they can see, to make them aware of how it relates to communication, and to accustom them to thinking of language as their own.

It is important at this point to clarify the parents' role in the language-acquisition process. As mentioned earlier, we do not encourage parents to function as language teachers. Teaching the structure of language, which is really its essence, is a skill that requires years of professional training. But we do believe that by accustoming themselves to think of language in visual terms, parents can begin exposing their children to language as soon as deafness is diagnosed or even suspected. In school, too, the emphasis must be not on speech, which is too often the main focus in both oral and total communication programs, but on *language,* as presented in reading and writing as well as signing, fingerspelling, or speechreading, depending on the mode of communication decided upon.

Despite our protests that parents are not teachers, you might be asking yourself at this point how much responsibility you need to accept for teaching your child language. The harsh truth is reflected in the average reading levels of the deaf, cited earlier. Without the active support of their families in the learning of language, deaf children seem to have difficulty progressing beyond a certain point. By "support" here we mean the effort to make language available to the child all day long and to encourage the child to use language and to feel at home with it. Parents have a much greater opportunity than teachers to make language visible to their children: all day, from three o'clock on, when the hearing child would ordinarily be drenched in the language of the home and neighborhood, deaf children need the same exposure, though through the alternative means of the eyes.

Unfortunately, in many households deaf children do not receive this kind of support for language learning. We believe the reason for this is that many parents remain unaware of the need for making language visible. To gain an understanding of visible language yourself, simply think about it while driving down a moderately busy street. What is the first thing you notice? Well, the traffic lights, for one thing—these do not reflect visual language per se, but they do make the principle of visual communication clear and could serve as an example to a deaf child of how symbolic language works. Red goes on and everyone agrees to stop; green goes on and everyone agrees to go. Thus, symbolically, red *means* stop; green *means* go.

Now, look at the WAIT/WALK sign at the pedestrian crosswalk. In some areas, the WAIT sign is not only a word but also an open hand —which is really a picture demonstration of the concept it conveys. Such a sign could be used in the same way picture books are, by creating an association between a single word and a picture.

But keep driving—what do you see? Street signs, store signs, license plates, words painted on the street, road signs. Language is visible everywhere. Hearing people tend to take for granted the words that guide them through their towns, but for deaf children, each sign, each word—FIRE DEPARTMENT, POLICE, LIBRARY, FISH MARKET—could, were the children's attention drawn to it, reinforce an understanding of what language is and how it works.

Naming Objects

Begin as you would with a hearing child, by naming objects. Again we find ourselves in the position of stating the obvious, since many parents fail to realize that it is possible to feed language to the very young deaf child and are instead swept by feelings of futility at the thought of making the effort. Now, when the child is six, twelve, eighteen months old, or whatever age at which the deafness has been discovered, the time is right to pull down the dike that stands between the child and the sea of language.

The idea is *to weld words to things and actions* right from the beginning and to create links in the child's mind between the things in his or her world and words. This means, for instance, pointing to a ball and saying or signing "ball," or indicating yourself and saying or signing "mama" or "papa." The initial purpose is to imbue the child with an intuitive understanding of the function of words, which act as symbols for things or actions.

The question naturally arises as to how you are to "say" these words to the very young deaf child. Theoretically, you would use the mode of communication—oral or total communication methods—that you have chosen to pursue both in your home and in the course of your child's education. In the very first months after discovery, however, you might not have decided firmly on a mode of communication. There is no question that making such a decision involves time-consuming research and soul-searching. Thus, during the interim period when you remain undecided or when you have decided on total communication but have not yet begun to learn sign language (though you should start a course *as soon* as you decide and should begin signing immediately, no matter how few signs you know at first), we encourage you to make words visible by means of speech, the element shared by both oralism and total communication. Point to objects and speak the word directly to the baby's eyes—make sure your lips are at the child's eye level *whenever* you speak. Remember: You are making the word *visible* to the child. In a total communication household, add signs as you learn them.

It is important that you speak the words naturally at all times, for a number of reasons. First, your spoken word, though directed at the eyes, could be entering the ears as well. We have noted that determining the level of a very young hearing-impaired child's residual hearing is usually impossible; thus, the child might well be hearing some of your words or some parts of them. We want children who can hear to learn to distinguish the sounds of normal speech, though amplified. Therefore, keeping your speech natural is important. But the same is true for speaking to the eyes. We want our children to learn to read words as spoken normally in the world at large, not artifically distorted by shouting or by grossly exaggerated pronounciation. Therefore, speak clearly, make sure nothing is impeding the child's view of your lips—such as smoking, gum chewing, or a moustache in need of trimming—and remain intent on making the words visible as they are spoken in everyday conversation among hearing people.

The process of naming objects and actions—"ball," "mama," "milk," "eat," "carry," "sleep"—is the first step in building receptive language in both hearing and deaf children. In the first year of life the child basically *receives* a vocabulary. Anyone who has raised a hearing child knows that children collect and store up language for many months before they start to use words to express themselves. Thus, in visibly naming through speaking or signing, pointing, and making explicit the relationships between words and their referents, parents of deaf children are enabling the child to store up the tools necessary for using language expressively. Where parents fail to make the effort to duplicate this in-rushing of words, which hearing children experience effortlessly during all their waking hours, deaf children simply do not have enough experience with language to progress normally in learning to understand and use it.

Once you feel comfortable with the naming process, you might proceed to easy word games to teach words through discrimination. Use two objects—say, a ball and a shoe—and communicate the words for each; then ask the child to discriminate between them: "Give me the ball"; then, "Give me

the shoe." As time goes on and you feel that the child has
made the connections, add a third element to the game.

The Written Word

Simultaneously with speaking or signing words, you can
feed the growing vocabulary by labeling objects around the
house. The slight concession in home decorating you'll make
in plastering the house with clearly written labels will be more
than compensated for by the association your child will eventually make between the written words and certain familiar
objects. Several teachers familiar with the language problems
deaf children commonly experience urged us to suggest that all
labels contain articles—"*the* stove," "*a* chair," "*the* sofa," "*a*
window"—rather than nouns alone, since deaf people poorly
grounded in language often have a lifelong difficulty using articles correctly in their expressive language. These same teachers encourage parents to change labels to simple sentences as
the child grows older, perhaps at age four or five.

It's important to state strongly here that one can go overboard with labeling and naming. Language is much more than
a long list of words, but even many teachers lay too much
stress on vocabulary without progressing steadily toward sentence construction. In one famous study in which four and one
half million words from popular magazines were counted and
classified, it was revealed that only twenty-five words account-
ed for approximately 33 percent of the total, appearing one
and one half million times. Thus, an individual doesn't need an
extensive vocabulary to read. What one does need to use language properly is the ability to construct sentences. Thus,
make the transition from single words to simple sentence construction as soon as the child has enough words to make this
possible. The progression will not only aid the child in gaining
a sense of sentence structure but will provide a context for new
vocabulary words and demonstrate their usage more clearly
than presentation of the words as words alone.

A blackboard in a central place, perhaps near the dinner table where most family discussions take place, should be an institution in your home. From the time your child can focus on a written word—and, again, long before you would introduce a hearing child to writing—make new words available to your deaf child by printing them clearly on the blackboard, speaking them clearly, and making the association explicit between the word, written and spoken or signed, and the object or action you are referring to. The use of the blackboard at mealtime has the added advantage of drawing the deaf child into the table talk from a very early age, whereas often during family meals deaf children are left out of lively discussions or are left behind. A child who isn't included soon loses the desire to participate. A blackboard can serve as an automatic reminder that the deaf child can and should enter the conversation, if only given the tools, made visible on the board. As the child grows older, parents can make use of the dictionary, learning enough about individual words, for example, to show syllable breaks and where the accent falls. Paul's father had a particular interest in the sources of words and took pleasure in conveying them to his deaf son once Paul was a teenager. Thus, *hippopotamus* was blocked out on the board and its Greek sources shown to be the words for river horse. In this way, language itself became a subject of interest.

Labeling and installing a blackboard should be the start of a lifelong habit of writing. Parents of hearing children rarely write much with their children, but with deaf children writing is an indispensable form of visible language. Where it is a part of the everyday interaction in the home, deaf children have the opportunity to take writing for granted from the start as a means of both receiving and conveying messages. Therefore, even for young children unable to read on their own, letters and postcards written to them personally by family members or friends cannot help but reinforce an understanding of the ways in which writing and language function—not to mention delighting the child with the pleasure of a personal communication.

A reservation is in order here. Despite the need to make lan-

guage visible, it is equally important to keep the environment
as natural as possible, being careful not to create situations in
which any member of your household, including yourself,
might feel self-conscious. Too many obvious tools of learning
around the home might bother your deaf child or other children. If so, find other, less obtrusive ways of making words
visible to your child.

Self-consciousness can become a problem in other ways, too.
Scott, for instance, profoundly deaf from birth, suffered awful
embarrassment throughout his childhood, for his father felt
compelled whenever there was company to force Scott to show
off his accomplishments. Thus, the boy would be prodded and
cajoled into standing up in front of the family's guests, all
properly quieted, to demonstrate his new words, his pronunciation, his comprehension. These sessions were humiliating for
Scott and probably made the guests uneasy as well. Moral: Be
alert to the effect of your enthusiasm.

Picture Games

A mail-order catalogue or a load of magazines can provide
an endless game for stimulating the child's use of symbols and
their relationships to words. Cut out and paste pictures of animals on cardboard and get the child to group them—birds in a
pile, dogs in another, cows in a third—so the child can gain
experience in the meaning of the words marking each category. One mother we know who played this sorting game with
her three-year-old deaf boy had the chance to indulge in a real
burst of pride when a hearing visitor, four years old and fasci-
nated with the game, called all the four-legged animals "dog,"
regardless of whether they were horses, cows, or sheep, whereas her little boy, through long practice, had all the names of
the groups.

The final stage of the animal-sorting game ought to be a visit to a farm, where the child can make the mental leap from
picture symbol and word to the real-life animal. Remember,

the idea is to weld words with experience. Pictures themselves are symbols, and children need to be shown the things pictures represent.

Story Reading

We've noted elsewhere that books have the potential to supply deaf people with all they miss auditorally—but only if as children deaf people learn to feel comfortable enough with books to seek them out. Clearly, the low average reading level among the deaf is tragic for the very reason that it cuts them off from a world of information and pleasure that, with good language skills, they could enjoy with complete independence. Plainly, the goal of putting deaf children at ease with books from an early age is reason enough to make story reading a nightly ritual.

The other benefit of reading to the child is that it combines all the elements identified so far—pictures, written language, and the chosen visible communication mode—to feed the child's need for visible language. Many educators feel that consistently reading to deaf children alone can be a decisive factor in the development of their language skills. As nowhere else, in a story—shown in pictures, written words, the speech or signs of the reader, and the reader's facial and body language—the child is immersed in language made visible on many levels. The very simplest stories for young children serve to convey images or to relate single words to single images. In stories of the next level of complexity, the structure of English becomes apparent in simple sentences, and the child is exposed to it even while engaged in the story. In the same way that hearing children learn the structure of language—that is, the correct way to string separate kinds of words together to form understandable messages—by constant auditory exposure to statements, questions, commands, exclamations, so deaf children can gain exposure to these patterns painlessly by being shown story upon story upon story. Later, in school, both deaf and hearing children are taught to focus explicitly on the structure and word order of English, and deaf children in particular must work hard to gain command of this knowledge. But how much further ahead deaf children will be if they already have a familiarity with the structure of the language when they enter school, gained through years of bedtime story reading.

One family serves as a good example. John, the father, began reading to his son, Isaac, from the time the boy was ten months old. At sixteen months, Isaac was diagnosed as profoundly deaf, and the news seemed to deepen John's resolve to make storytime a nightly ritual. He continued using the body-language techniques he had used from the beginning—in a sad story, using his fingers to show tears on his cheeks; in a happy one, showing excitement. He was completely uninhibited about miming stories to Isaac. At eleven, after being exposed to these visible stories—through pictures, print, mime, and, in his case, signs—for nearly ten and a half years, Isaac reads at an amazing eighth-grade level. John says with a smile that he fully intends to read to Isaac nightly until the boy is twenty-one.

Reading old, familiar stories time and again has its own rewards, since repetition provides the child with the chance to think about the deep structure of language. The first three or four times through, perhaps, the child might be focused solely on the tale, whereas on the fourth time through he or she might notice something—the form of a word, the structure of a phrase—that makes him or her think about language itself.

As the child grows older, increasing not only the number but the kinds of books available is of great value. Two reasons for introducing a wide range of topics are interrelated. First, mysteries, animal books, sports books, science books, and western books, for example, all introduce their own special vocabularies, words that crop up only in their contexts. The more that specialized categories are opened to the deaf child, the more freely he or she will range through the language as a whole. In a language sense, new vocabularies open up new realms of experience. The same is true for hearing children, of course, but in the context of familiarizing deaf children with language, the need for variety has a special meaning.

The second benefit of exposure to a variety of types of books relates to the fact that deaf children frequently have difficulty comprehending abstract concepts, as opposed to concrete word-thing or word-action associations. In part, a poor comprehension of abstractions comes from a lack of experience, which in turn results from a limited exposure to language. In the past, many parents and teachers have had such low expectations of deaf children's abilities to acquire language that they have restricted exposure to language for fear of overwhelming the children. As in most cases of lowered expectations, the children tend to remain well within predicted limits.

Our plea is that parents bring any and every realm of experience into their children's lives via books. We believe that exposure can never hurt, and that it can result in the child's insight into what's involved in, say, solving a crime, breaking in a horse, reporting a story—abstract concepts that he or she might not be exposed to in daily life. Even more certain is that the child will gain familiarity with adjectives and adverbs in different contexts. Adjectives and adverbs, modifying words, have also been identified as troublesome for many deaf people. Keeping a variety of books, especially as the child grows older, will ensure that he or she sees modifying words used often and applied to many different situations.

A hint to parents of deaf children seven and up: comic books, with their mixture of action-oriented pictures and fast-paced dialogue, are well suited for children beginning to read on their own for pleasure but perhaps intimidated by pages of straight type. The content of most comics leaves a lot to be desired, but the classic comic books, for instance, in which classics of literature are told in comic-book form, are appropriate. The funny comics, too, as opposed to the gory crime and violence types, offer children opportunities to explore stories on their own. Parents have to monitor comic reading, though, to make sure their children are really reading, instead of merely skimming along on the cartoons.

Scrapbooks

Home-made books can have inestimable value in focusing the child's interest on language. Start off simply, with pictures and two-word labels. But don't confine yourself to magazine and catalogue pictures here; get hold of a Polaroid camera and teach yourself *and* your child how to use it. Use the camera to record family experiences and the book to relate these experiences to visible language. Preschoolers, for example, will enjoy mixing pictures of farm animals plus labels—"A COW," "A SHEEP," "A HORSE"—with snapshots of their own and friends' domestic animals—"OUR DOG, POLLY," "JANE, THE KITTEN."

The scrapbook can come to serve as a memory enforcer to be used with, say, trips to the farm or zoo. Helping your child to arrange labels with cut-out pictures of animals in a book might be the first step in a plan to visit a farm to see the animals. At the farm you would take your own pictures to be matched with the ones in the book at home. This exercise has a double value: it gives the child the opportunity to see how language relates to real-life experience, and it also helps the child begin to use language *to record* his or her personal experience. Deaf children need practice in relating their personal memories to language; remembering in words is a form of abstract thinking. By returning again and again to a book made at home that actually shows that special trip to the farm, the zoo, the park, or even the market or a neighbor's house, the child not only learns to recognize new words but relates those words to memory.

The scrapbook can and should become more complex as the child grows older, recording not just vocabulary words but simple sentences as well. Whereas story reading can be viewed as a means of encouraging the development of the receptive side of language—that is, the understanding of language—the scrapbook can be used to help the expressive side—the use of language—to grow. Long descriptions of the pictures aren't necessary, nor are long paragraphs, but short sentences, describing not only the subject of the picture but also the dominant feeling of the experience it conveys—"WE WENT TO THE MARKET. WE ALL FELT TIRED." "WE VISITED A SCHOOL. JERRY LOVED THE TOYS."—can help children to understand the power they can have over language in expressing themselves.

Scrapbooks can help to solve a couple of practical problems that might otherwise pose difficulties for deaf children and their families. The first is the identification of family members, both by name and relationship. Deaf children need visual input on names in order to remember them, and they often don't get enough to keep everyone straight, especially absent aunts, uncles, and cousins. Using pictures and picture groupings can also help to explain what an aunt is, what a cousin is, even, for a very young only child, what a brother or sister is. Thus, it's much easier to show how Jim, *here,* and Bill, *here,* both have the same mother, *here,* than to explain the abstract concept *brother* in speech or signs alone.

Children who are old enough to be learning to spell love to see the names of their friends spelled out, so this is another way to use the scrapbook. Seeing a friend's name printed out for the first time can give the child a special thrill. And, of course, from an early age the child should be made familiar with his or her own full name, address, and phone number.

The guiding principle behind the scrapbook is that it relates visible language to the child's own realm of experience. Hearing children learn languages by interacting with it during practically all their waking hours, not by memorizing lists of words that have nothing to do with their daily lives. Deaf children can do the same, but language must be made available to them. In the scrapbook, full of pictures with personal meanings for the child, words and sentence structures can be welded with experience to become meaningful.

Writing Tasks

As soon as the child begins to have the motor control to manipulate a writing tool, usually at around age four, the child
should begin to think of writing as a means of verbal expression. You can encourage a familiarity with writing by inviting
the child to make labels—with his or her own name and with
parents' and siblings' names. Older children might be invited
to address a letter, make a shopping list, and of course write
contributions to the scrapbook—any job that puts writing to a
meaningful use.

Other forms of self-expression—painting, drawing, finger-
painting, calligraphy—are important, too. All such activities
can serve to link the inner person with the outside world. The
point is to keep that pathway unobstructed all the time. The
more means a child has for self-expression the better.

Preschool Games

Playing the same games with your deaf preschooler as you
would with hearing toddlers is imperative. We only mention
this necessity here because many parents, in discouragement,
fail to realize that playing such games is not only possible with
deaf children but can be a source of certain kinds of information. For example, where else will children learn the parts of
their face and body except through that old standby, "Where
is your . . . nose?" "Where is your . . . mouth?" Remember,
communicate directly to the child's eyes, speaking or signing,
whatever is your choice, and play often with the certainty that
you are feeding your child the information he or she craves.

Do the same with colors and with qualities—for example,
rough versus smooth textures, clean versus dirty hands, fast
versus slow walking. And play counting games, too. With this
sort of play you are laying the groundwork for the child's vocabulary by relating words to direct experience. Words gain
meaning when they replace, recall, or explain situations. By
pouring words into your child's awareness via the eyes, you
will be building the foundation for all language-oriented be-

havior—reading, writing, speaking, signing, and, most fundamental of all, thinking.

Letter Blocks and Games

By age two and a half children are interested in individual
letters. Make sure you keep easily manipulated letters and
numbers around the house—alphabet blocks, felt boards, letter
puzzles, and plastic letters are a few of the letter toys available.
Young children are particularly enchanted by magnetic letters
that stick to the surface of refrigerators. Also, as soon as the
child shows an interest, include an alphabet book in the nightly reading ritual.

Building Language Awareness

We've mentioned how useful road signs and store signs can
be for conveying to the child the significance of language.
Point out instances wherever you are—at the market, on the
bus, and so on. In the home, too, there are many opportunities
to make the child aware of the importance of print—show him
or her labels, newspapers, the phone book, cookbooks, and the
address book.

Activities Involving Language

Cooking and shopping are two examples of household activities that involve language. Drawing deaf children into such
activities not only exposes them to specialized vocabularies—
for example, of measurements, cooking techniques, names of
foods, prices, denominations of currency—but once again reinforces the idea of the importance of printed language in daily
life. The third benefit, of course, lies in the child's pleasure at
participating and interacting in a productive activity.

Sports, too, have their own vocabularies as well as their own
rules and procedures, which are expressed in words. Linking
pleasurable activities with words can only result in more experience for the child with language, its vocabulary and structure.

Calendars and Maps

Both calendars and maps are visual representations of abstract concepts, the former of time, the latter of distance. The idea of time in particular dominates daily life. To enable your child to develop an accurate sense of time passing and an understanding of the units of time—days, weeks, months, and years—keep a large, simple-to-read calendar at the child's eye level.* The fill-in type is best, since you will be able to mark down important events and thus build a visible record of the past. This simple device can also serve to keep the child informed about family plans that he or she might miss news of otherwise.

Maps, too, make a difficult idea visible, and they have the added advantage of familiarizing the child with new words, both geographical names and words denoting units of distance. Even for short distances, children can get pleasure from tracing a trip on a map, and deaf children will benefit—as will hearing children, of course—from using a tool in which words and graphics are shown together.

Collecting Things

Collecting anything—stamps, pictures, dolls, flowers—can benefit deaf children simply by connecting them to the world. True enthusiasts soon begin to read about their collectibles, so for deaf children an added advantage of collecting is the motivation to read, independent of parents or teachers. And as with cooking or sports, a specialized interest brings with it its own vocabulary and set of written symbols. Coins, for example, carry various letters indicating where they were minted, and stamps are distinguished by a world of different words and letters.

---

*Dormac, Inc. supplies high-quality learning materials (calendars, workbooks, and the like) to teachers and parents of children with disabilities. For information, write Dormac, Inc., P.O. Box 752, Beverton, Oregon 97075 or call (503) 641-3128.

Making Up Stories and Making Believe

Encourage your child to make up stories with you or with siblings. Deaf children often make stilted "formula" sentences, based on the rigid patterns they learn by memory in school language lessons. At home, outside the atmosphere of diligent study, we can encourage them to explore the language they possess and to make it work with their imaginations. Even by asking them for a response here and there to a familiar story— "What color was Goldilocks's hair? YELLOW!!" "Why couldn't she eat the porridge at first? IT WAS TOO HOT!!"— we are asking them to jump into the story and use their language powers to enhance the fun.

Playing make-believe is effective for the same reason. Many parents are overly serious with their deaf children, driven by worry and concern for the future. But much is to be gained by relaxing and letting playfulness take over. A very specific problem is addressed by pretending, too, since many deaf people fail ever to gain mastery over the subjunctive mood in English, the construction that conveys the idea of "if"—"If I were king, I would . . ."; "If I were a boy, I would. . . ." Pretending is a real-life exercise in the subjunctive mood. The more experience deaf children have with "if," the greater are their chances of understanding and expressing themselves in this complex English construction.

Role playing, or pretending, also benefits deaf children in allowing them to explore different moods and feelings and to find names for these subjective states. People whose command of language is weak are frequently unable to express their feelings because they have no names for them. Deaf children with poor language skills often have no means at all of making sense of their feelings, simply because they lack the vocabulary to do so. The traditional result is the tantrum—an explosion of chaotic emotions that conveys little specific information about what the child is feeling and why. In a make-believe game, parents can guide children in exploring various feelings and can provide the vocabulary for expressing them: "Oh, little

boy, your mommy went away. You must be sad and lonely";
or "I'm angry. Grr. That lion took my place"; or "Why are
you crying, bunny? Did you lose your carrot?"

Sound Games and Songs

Parents and teachers alike often consider sounds, for example, barnyard sounds—moos, clucks, baas, and neighs—to be
outside the realm of deaf children. But why shouldn't deaf
children learn the sounds that animals and things make? The
ways in which other beings communicate and the sounds
things make in the everyday world constitute a significant aspect of our experience, and there is no reason to justify deaf
people being cut off from such information. Again, such
sounds must be made accessible by being made visible, say,
with a picture of a cow plus a "moo" plus the spoken or fingerspelled word; or with a picture of an airplane plus a "var-
oom" plus mime to convey the intensity of the sound.

Singing, too, offers sources of pleasure and stimulation.
Deaf children can feel rhythm and the vibration of instruments, responding to and experiencing music on a different
level than hearing people, and can enjoy dancing fully as much
as the nonhearing-impaired. They can sing also, both vocally
and through sign language—exploring the novel phenomena
of rhyme and matched rhythms encountered elsewhere only in
poetry—outside the rigid framework of classroom language
lessons.

Word Games

Word games offer practice, disguised as fun, in various aspects of language use. Many good commercial word games are
sold, and many other games that incorporate words or written
instructions but are not specifically designed as word games
can be useful as well. Games you invent yourself or borrow
from another source can also be very effective language exercises, and free and fun as well. The best part about word games
is that they can be adapted to give practice in particular lan-

guage problems, enabling you to focus on your child's trouble areas without nagging or being discouraging.

One simple game for young children will be familiar to all ex-public schoolers: Simon Says. Simon Says is a command game; the players must do what the leader instructs them to do, but only if the leader says "Simon says" before each command: "Simon says, wiggle your foot; Simon says, bend your arm; nod your head; Simon says, run around the room." In this case, the head nodders would be out. The great value of this game for deaf children is that it requires the player to attend to *all* parts of the message, not just the subject and object, which is a common bad habit among deaf children.

For preschoolers, an even easier homemade game might be simple groupings: What animals fly? What animals swim? What says baaa? What says moo? Very young children need practice in classifying and naming. Again, we urge you to play the same games with your deaf preschooler that you would with hearing children of the same age.

For children who know colors, what about those old, on-the-road license-plate games designed to drive parents mad? "How many blue plates can you find? When you see one shout, 'Kadiddle.' " Or to encourage the development of a sense of time: "How many blue plates can you spot in ten minutes—when the big hand gets to the two?"

The possibilities for games are endless. What you play and how much you play will depend to some extent on your inventiveness and patience, or on those of the other children in your household. But whatever games you play, the hope is that while your child is participating, his or her experience with language will be increasing. The objective is to encourage the child to take possession of language naturally, as hearing children do, and through familiarity to feel comfortable with it.

APPROACHING PROBLEM AREAS

In the preceding sections, we have implied that certain specific stumbling blocks are common among deaf children in their understanding and expressive use of language. Because language is profoundly complex, and because most people lack extensive training in the structure of language, parents are rarely aware of these specific problem areas. We believe, however, that parents can profit immeasurably from an awareness of the problems deaf people traditionally have with language simply by becoming less likely to unknowingly reinforce bad habits in their children. Such parents might even be able to counteract errors to some extent by consciously serving as good language models. Because a good grasp of language is essential to all the child's communication skills, and because up to now the record in teaching deaf children language has been notably poor, we feel that a deepened understanding on the part of parents could help turn the tide toward a firm language mastery among deaf children.

Still, it is important to emphasize once again that parents should not view themselves as language teachers, or as teachers at all. Parents have a big enough job without taking on the responsibilities of language specialists. What parents can and must do, however, is to make the tools of language acquisition available to their children. This general task includes choosing a mode of communication, choosing a school in which language receives proper attention, and providing a home environment in which language learning is encouraged and reinforced. Included in the latter condition is the idea that family members provide a good language model and make visible that sea of words that is necessary to the child's success.

Two more warnings are in order before we turn to specific language problems. First, no matter how many errors you detect in your child's particular message, and no matter how strong is the urge to correct the child on the spot, be careful never to discourage communication. If you understand the gist of the child's message despite the errors, make it clear that you have understood *before* you focus on the problems. The child needs to know that he or she has fulfilled the main function of communication in getting the message across. To ignore the success of the child's effort in the haste to focus on the failures is to risk suggesting, silently and inadvertently, that the whole endeavor isn't worth the struggle. Many, many deaf children stop progressing in their language learning between ages seven and eight. We want to counteract this pattern, whatever its causes, at all costs. We believe that the essential first step in keeping deaf children engaged in language is to provide an atmosphere of positive encouragement.

The second warning is this: When you have a correction to make—and this applies whenever you teach a deaf child anything, under any circumstances—break down your message into the smallest possible units and present these units one at a time. Deaf children learn by mastering bits of information; they are overwhelmed by complex explanations, for usually their language is not complete enough to allow them to follow. Parents and teachers, in their eagerness—or impatience, or anxiety—too often crush children's spirits under the weight of too heavy, too complex explanations.

Related to this warning is another hint about presenting information. Some people characteristically try to correct or teach deaf children by repeating the same sentence, or even the same word, over and over again. Often, they change their intonation or emphasis but keep the construction of their message the same. Remember, if a deaf child doesn't understand your message, spoken, signed, or fingerspelled, reconstruct it. Repeating yourself over and over will lead to nothing but frustration on both sides.

One particular function that parents of language-acquiring children perform naturally is known technically as *expansion.* Expansion is the process of repeating the child's message back in expanded and corrected form. Thus, if a child communicates the message "Mama, ball" and points, you might indicate that you have understood but still take the opportunity to expand the message by communicating, "The ball is rolling away." Again, if the child forms the message "Me, candy," you would nod to indicate your comprehension and, in correct language, communicate the expanded "Oh, you want some candy." You don't have to demand that the child repeat the correct message; rather, make sure you repeat the message correctly so the child can see it. Too often, parents miss the chance to reflect good language because they are content merely to respond to the child's message as long as they understand it. They tend to mentally fill in the blanks in the child's message.

Expansion can apply to stretching the child's capacity and is not necessarily limited to correcting errors. Thus, when a child communicates the message "Dad, I want my shoes," you have the opportunity to enrich the construction by asking, "Which shoes do you want, the blue or the black shoes?" Simply adding adjectives to a bland message is an easy and useful form of expansion.

Verbs

The many forms of verbs—action words—cause difficulties because the forms are numerous and the reasons for changes in form are very subtle. Hearing children learn to make the various changes in verb form through constant exposure long before they go to school and memorize the rules governing these changes. But deaf children are often deprived of exposure to these forms, frequently because parents feel tempted to simplify when communicating with them.

Tense

Thus, deaf children commonly exhibit problems with verb *tense* (that is, *when* the action is taking place as indicated by the verb form), for example:

> I want
> I wanted
> I will want
> I have wanted

Deaf children have particular difficulties with the tense changes of the verb *to be*. The words that represent the various

form of *to be* have no obvious meaning in themselves and have
to be learned by experience alone:

> I am
> you are
> I was
> you were
> I, you will be
> I, you have been

Give these tenses back to your child in expanded constructions
whenever appropriate, instead of allowing errors to become
permanently ingrained habits. Tense changes are important to
the meaning of messages, and an imperfect understanding of
them could significantly reduce your child's understanding
and effectiveness in communicating.

Mood: Subjunctive

The mood of a verb is the manner of doing or being expressed by the form of a verb. The mood most frequently troublesome to the deaf is the subjunctive mood, the form that
expresses a wish or a condition improbable or contrary to fact.

> If I were a boy, I'd cut my hair.
> If I were a dog, I'd be a collie.

As we mentioned earlier, pretending or playing make-believe is
a way of expanding not language specifically but experience
that can give meaning to certain language constructions. In
this case, the idea of "what if" gives the child experience in the
reasoning behind the subjunctive mood and therefore creates a
reason for using it.

Voice: Active versus Passive

The *voice* of a verb expresses whether the subject of the sentence acts (the active voice) or is acted upon (passive voice).
For example:

> The truck hit the car. (active)
> The truck was hit by the car. (passive)

Deaf people often fail to perceive the difference between these two sentences and interpret the two as identical. In games with objects that act and are acted upon, you can address this common confusion before it takes hold. Make a habit of visibly identifying the actor and the receiver of the action.

Nouns and Pronouns
Pronouns

People inexperienced in the English language often have trouble using pronouns:

> *he* for Bill
> *she* for Mary
> *them* for Mary and Jane

and in identifying the people referred to by pronouns in another's message. A deaf child might form the following constructions:

> Mary, Bill come to school.
> Mary, Bill carry my books.

Such a message is crying out for an expansion such as "Oh, they carried your books? How nice."

Articles

Another common problem related to noun use is the dropping of articles: *the, a, an.* Thus, common usages among deaf people might be

> Throw ball.
> I want orange.

It is to increase familiarity with articles that we have urged that all household labels and captions in scrapbooks contain the articles along with the nouns.

Conjunctions in Compound Nouns

Many deaf people have trouble manipulating conjunctions, or connecting words, between nouns and often drop them in constructing messages. Thus, whereas the correct construction would be

> Mom *and* Dad are going to the zoo

a common error might be

> Mom, Dad going to zoo.

All the problems cited in this section involving nouns are easy to spot and simple to counteract in correctly constructed expansions.

Noun/Verb Agreement

One of the most basic grammar rules in English is that the subject and verb of a sentence must agree in form. When the subject is singular, the verb form must be singular; when the subject is plural, so must be the verb form. Thus,

> Bill and Jane were cold. (not *was* cold)
> I am going. (not I *are*).

Deaf people need constant practice in noun/verb agreement, for the correct matching forms are not self-evident and must be learned by experience.

Plurals

Typically, deaf people with poor language skills cut corners. The dropping of conjunctions, mentioned above, is one way of doing this. Failing to use plural forms of nouns where plurals are indicated is another, as in

> I want two candy.
> He (meaning *they*) go (meaning *went*) to the store.

This error is an easy one to ignore, but parents confident that their children can perfect their language skills will monitor for it carefully and give back the correct plural form through expansion wherever appropriate.

Word Order

The conventions of English word order make up another category of information that children learn nearly automatically, through experience, long before they come across them formally in school. Hearing children pick up the order and rhythm of English through constant exposure to speech. Deaf children, of course, need more explicit guidance in constructing sentences correctly. Perhaps above all in regard to word order, parents tend to be tolerant of errors when the meaning is clear—for example:

> Zoo, I want to go.
> Ice cream, me, I want.

But here more than ever a solid grounding through expansion of well-constructed sentences made visible can only result in more freedom to manipulate language effectively.

Sentence Types

Related to the problem of word order is that of distinguishing among types of sentences that perform specific functions. Statements, questions, and commands are distinct from each other in their form:

> Sammy isn't here. (statement)
> Who has seen Sammy? (question)
> Go and look for Sammy. (command)

Deaf children need practice in distinguishing among these forms and in constructing them themselves.

Comparatives and the Subtlety of Language

Deaf people frequently have difficulty with expressions of degrees, as in *big, bigger, biggest; blue, bluer, bluest;* and *some, many, most.* Using pictures to demonstrate the degree of given qualities can help children understand the differences among the words in these sets and the usefulness of the distinctions.

Making explicit the distinctions among comparatives relates

to a broader topic of great significance to language-learning deaf children: the subject of subtlety. Many usages, such as the comparative, and an infinite number of words have capabilities and connotations that are not immediately apparent in the single use of a word, or even in a grammar book or a dictionary. Once again, the subtlety of language—the appropriateness of certain constructions, the underlying meanings of certain words—is learnable only through exposure and experience. If your child is using a word inappropriately, he or she needs explicit information that few people will feel comfortable offering. For example, one man we know learned as a child "Thou shalt not kill" from the Bible and began to use "thou" and "you" interchangeably. Until his mother corrected him he had no way of knowing that this usage was archaic and inappropriate. Thus, an important part of your monitoring function is helping your child to gain experience in the subtle meanings of words and in specific constructions.

Modifiers

Adjectives and adverbs describe or add information about nouns and verbs, respectively. These modifying words present difficulties for deaf children because they generally convey abstract ideas, which are more difficult to learn than concrete ideas. For example, a ball can be red, round, smooth, dirty, big, and shiny. Conveying the word *ball* is a relatively easy matter of pointing to the ball and making the association with the word, but familiarizing the deaf child with each of the qualities listed is more complex, requiring that the child experience many instances of red, for example, to understand the essence of that quality. The same is true of adverbs:

I run slowly, poorly, crazily, jerkily. . . .
Pick up the rabbit gently, swiftly, sweetly, carefully. . . .

Simply realizing that learning the meaning of modifying words involves much experience will help you to devise games that first expose the child to the qualities expressed, then encourage the child to use such words correctly. A simple question-answer exercise that promotes this kind of learning could include such questions as "What do you do when you're hungry? What do you do when you're tired?" And reading, of course, is the great expander.

Another reason to work adjectives and adverbs into your communication is to enrich your child's language experience generally. In school, deaf children most often learn proper English sentence construction by formula—that is, they learn to plug words into formulas for various kinds of sentences. The result is often a stiff, formal habit of construction resulting in sentences that convey the bare minimum of information and are far from expressions of spontaneous thoughts and feelings. Parents have perhaps more opportunities in the course of daily living than do teachers in crowded classrooms to explore with their children the expressive potential of language. One crucial function parents can play, then, in monitoring their deaf children's language is to help the children enliven their language by gaining familiarity and practice with modifiers.

*   *   *

In conclusion, we repeat our initial warning. You are a parent, not a teacher. To attempt to take on the latter role would not only overburden you but perhaps would be a disservice to your child, as it could drain your energy away from more fundamental work as a parent. But in providing an atmosphere in which language is made visible, you will be making language available to your child on a full-time basis. Otherwise exposure might be limited to the few hours a day during which the child does language work in school.

Chapter 6

The School Environment

IN THE SECTION THAT FOLLOWS, we assume that your child is in school, at whatever grade level, from preschool through high school. You have settled on a mode of communication, selected a program, and now perceive your responsibility to be monitoring your child's progress and continually evaluating the program. At each semester break, as your child progresses through the system, you will doubtless feel the need to visit the new classroom and talk with the new teacher, much as you would tend to watch over a hearing child's schooling.

The special needs of your deaf child, however, make your continual evaluation of the school program perhaps more critical than with a hearing child. To be blunt, more can go wrong in a school program for deaf children, particularly in a public school where deaf children are integrated, or "mainstreamed," into regular classrooms with hearing children. In this situation, parents not only express their natural concern by monitoring closely but also protect their legal right to demand that all their children's educational needs, however special, be met.

We will look at mainstreaming in detail in the second half of this chapter. In this first section our purpose is to point out special conditions that must be met in a classroom in which deaf children are taught. These conditions apply to any classroom—be it in a special day school for the deaf, a residential school for the deaf, a special classroom for deaf students in a public school, or a regular classroom in which deaf students, or even one deaf student, have been integrated. The purpose of this section is to provide you with a checklist that you can use in a one- or two-hour-long visit to your child's classroom.

As we will explain in more detail later, under federal law handicapped children are entitled to a free education, equivalent in quality to that available to normal children and matched to their special needs. However, no one can serve as more effective advocates in securing the appropriate education for disabled children than the parents of those children. Furthermore, most education personnel involved with disabled students know that the key to maintaining the quality of their programs is the active participation of parents. Most teachers and administrators welcome and encourage parent advocacy and worry about those children whose parents passively accept their children's education without showing much concern or interest.

This chapter provides you with some specific tools for analyzing classrooms and teachers. It is possible that in so doing we will create the impression that parents must be aggressive in demanding high quality from a system that actively withholds it. The first part of this impression is true: Parents must be aggressive in demanding high quality. But for the most part, it should be remembered that teachers and administrators have the same interests as parents: providing high-quality education to their students and meeting the children's special needs. Most often, parents and teachers together face a common enemy: budget-conscious bureaucracy. Still, the battle against red tape and an ever-tightening budget does not wholly explain the need for aggressive parent participation. No matter how much your child's teachers, school counselors, and administrators care, their concern is for all their students, whereas yours is naturally for your own child first. Understand that the school personnel perceive you—or should perceive you—as your child's best advocate. Many educators actually despair at getting parents more involved in their children's education. They feel that the special problems of deafness in particular are poorly understood by society, especially by governmental funding agencies, largely because parents often misperceive the problems themselves and leave it to the educators to solve them.

For all these reasons, but most urgently for the sake of ensuring your child's full access to a good education, we urge you to request an hour or so of your child's teacher's time at the start of each school semester. Try to observe the class when it is in session and prepare to ask specific questions. Use the material in this section, but also ask yourself what you really need to know, both about the teacher's approach and your child's own progress. When you are dissatisfied, confused, or concerned, contact the program administrator but also broach the subject publicly in the school's parent-teacher association. By raising questions at the PTA, you will open the subject to public discussion, with a chance of gaining reassurance and new perspectives rather than relegating yourself to a long series of meetings in which you might find yourself feeling alone in your particular point of view.

THE CLASSROOM

We begin with some very basic considerations, which, surprisingly, even trained teachers of the deaf sometimes overlook.

Noise Level

Since auditory training is a significant factor in every education program for the deaf, regardless of the principal mode of communication, an auditory environment that interferes with the children's learning of sound discrimination is a serious impediment. Remember: Hearing aids amplify *all* sounds, not just speech. All the sounds in a noisy classroom might conceivably merge under amplification to mask the sounds, particularly speech sounds, that the children are trying to discern.

For this reason, the room should be designed and arranged with an eye to muting all extraneous sounds. Where outside noise is a problem, the air circulation system should permit windows to be closed. Carpets should cover the floor to reduce internal noise, and all equipment—film, slide, and filmstrip projectors—should be insulated to cut out the clicks and hums these machines usually generate. Acoustic tiles should line walls and ceilings, and glazed tiles and high-gloss paints should be scrupulously avoided.

If you find that your child's classroom is poorly designed as a learning environment for deaf children, remind the director of the program that insulating blankets or acoustic plasters are available for improving the acoustics of a room without retiling. The need for such a step becomes particularly apparent when one remembers that the energy both teachers and students spend in auditory training might be wasted due to a poor auditory environment. Depressingly, many teachers are unaware of—or perhaps over the years forget—the importance of reducing noise level. Thus, just by noting the quality of the auditory environment and looking for the ways in which the teacher has reduced noise level in the room, you will gain a sense of the particular teacher's sensitivities to the special needs of deaf children.

Lighting
Remember that deaf children receive most information through their eyes. Whether in an oral or a total communication program, they need a clear view of their teacher, the teacher's aide, and the other students in the room. An ideal setup would have windows on both sides of the room providing natural lighting evenly. Any ceiling fixtures would be attached not in the center of the ceiling, where they would tend to cast shadows on the faces of the people in the room, but around the sides of the room. Obviously, these ideal conditions

will not often be met, especially in regular public school classrooms. But teachers can be expected to set up a room to minimize glare and shadows and to maximize the visibility of everyone in the room.

Also remember that even where no views are obscured, a harsh glare tires not only the eyes but the whole body. Make note of the quality of the light, and if it is too harsh bring it to the attention of the teacher and/or the principal.

Seating Arrangements

The old convention of seating students in rows facing the blackboard just won't do for a class containing deaf students. Again, students need maximum visibility of teachers and of each other. Anyone whose face or hands are out of view may as well be out of the room. Thus, the best seating arrangement is an arclike one—a semicircle of students facing a teacher. Again, lighting is an important factor here. If the arc of students faces into a window or other light source, the teacher will be all but obliterated from view by the glare. Be sensitive to the setup of seats in relation to light sources, and check for blind spots in relation to students, teacher, and teacher's aides.

The Room's "Personality"

You can tell a lot about what happens in a classroom merely by stepping inside and absorbing the atmosphere. Usually this kind of assessment occurs at least partially on a subconscious level, but we urge you to sharpen your attention to the mood or "feel" of the room when familiarizing yourself with your child's educational environment.

We asked several supervisors of teachers of the deaf in elementary schools what they looked for when they entered a room to assess the effectiveness of the teacher. We reproduce some of their comments here in the hope that they will give you some leads in analyzing your own impressions:

> I want the room to reflect the person who put it together. After all, that teacher will spend most of his or her working

hours in that room and ought to want to feel comfortable there. I get worried if the classroom is "just right" but sterile. I wonder, "How much does that teacher care about bringing the things in that make him or her happy in this environment?" There are rooms like that. You walk in and see nothing. Anyone could walk in and be the teacher. It makes you wonder how much they care, how much they're prepared to give.

I want to see visuals galore, done well and cheerfully—but not overbusy and wild looking. The whole thrust in education of the deaf is making language and information visible. One of the things I'm assessing is the ability of the teacher to give information in a clear, visual way. We want the children to be able to glance up and receive incidental learning (like the stuff hearing children overhear without necessarily focusing on it). We want the material that's on the walls to reflect specific information or lessons that are being taught. When the children gaze around the room looking up from their work, they should be able to review something familiar to them or to have a lesson reinforced. They should be able to pick up information from the environment on their own. But we don't want them drowning in it. There has to be a balance.

*   *   *

I'm particularly looking for *language* made visible in the classroom, and language at the appropriate level for the students there. Parents will undoubtedly have trouble discerning the appropriateness of the level of language presented, but they should start to feel wary if they see little or no language posted on the boards.

Another thing I want to know is whether the teacher uses instructional media effectively. Is the overhead projector covered with dust, or is it clear that the teacher uses it daily to present information? The idea is to determine whether the teacher knows how to present information quickly and visually in a number of different ways. Though language is a chief concern, especially in the early years, we don't want the teacher depending on speech and speechreading or sign language or reading and writing alone. Rather we want the teacher to present the material in a variety of ways.

*   *   *

The worst room I was ever in had an intense glare with nothing to soften it. There was not one living thing in the room except people—no plants, no animals, no fish, and this was a first-grade classroom. Worse, there were no comfortable places in the room, no places where you could sit down and hang out and not worry about working. There was one work table, but nothing to indicate that creative work went on there—no puzzles or paints or anything like that. Basically the kids just sat in that room with their hands folded. I wasn't surprised to discover that the teacher relied almost solely on rote as a teaching technique—the teacher spoke and signed, the children responded as a group. The whole environment, the whole approach, was boring.

*   *   *

I look for activity and learning centers in the classrooms. Is the room just posted with displays for incidental learning, or are there areas in the room where kids can go off and work independently, privately? Maybe it's just a study carrel, or maybe a place where the child does arts and crafts. You'll see a list of directions over it: "Would you like to make something today? Follow these steps. . . ." Or maybe there's a nature corner with plants, animals, or a microscope. But most important of all for deaf children is the library corner—a place where they can sit down and read during free time, a place jammed with lots of books at all different levels. Library corners—I don't see them all the time, but I wish I did.

*   *   *

I always want to see a schedule when I go into a room. If I don't see one I get worried. Somewhere in the room I want to see a schedule, and big, so it's not the teacher's schedule but there for everybody in the room—visitors, aides, students—anyone who comes in can see the schedule. But I like to see a schedule that you can tell has been changed a lot to show it's adaptable, not too rigid. I don't like to come in and see that the only schedule is on the teacher's desk, a private thing for the teacher alone to refer to. One of the problems I run into a lot with young adult deaf people is a poor concept of scheduling and of time. I believe it's the result of a lack of experience—of not enough responsibility for meeting their own obligations. That's why I want to see them in the classroom saying, "Oh, it's 9:30, I'm supposed to. . . ." I still want to see the teacher, involved with the kids in discussion, saying, "Stay where you are, let's finish this, don't worry about the time." But still the schedule is very important.

Along the same lines and equally important is the job chart. There should be jobs in the room that the kids like to do or need to do even if they don't enjoy them. This means everyone's sharing the work—it's not all falling onto the shoulders of the teacher or the aide—and the children are learning and practicing appropriate behavior. The responsibility should be divided up on a chart visibly, with the names shiftable from job to job.

*   *   *

I'm a very strong disciplinarian. I don't believe in kids running pell-mell in the room. It bothers me to see kids coming into the room from a play break and throwing things and generally continuing their outside playing. I look for the children to understand the difference between a work and play environment. They don't necessarily have to line up and be regimented but just recognize where play and work occur.

THE TEACHER
Again, evaluating a teacher's performance, especially on the basis of one- or two-hour-long observation visits, is largely a matter of analyzing your impressions, particularly of the teacher's sensitivity to the special problems of deafness. Often, the most convincing information about teacher effectiveness will come from your child—is he or she happy with the teacher, is the relationship a productive one, and is the child progressing satisfactorily? Still, you can arm yourself with a number of specific questions that will help focus your impressions relating to the special conditions a child's deafness imposes on the process of teaching in the classroom.

What are the teacher's expectations of the children in the class?

This question comes first because we believe that if you think children will fail, you will communicate your expectation to them and, sure enough, they'll fail. Not all will fail, perhaps, but those unable to progress without outside encouragement will not find the boost they need. It is not necessarily implied that if you think the children will succeed, then they will succeed. But we feel safe in assuming that most children—most people of any age—will be more likely to stretch their capacities and try harder when a caring, thoroughly involved teacher is encouraging them than when they are working at a task under the eye of a teacher who considers their efforts—and his or her own—in vain.

Thus, we want our children's teachers to set high standards for our children and for themselves. If you sense discouragement or resignation—"The child is hopeless in language; I wouldn't expect any gain"; "This group has never had a grasp of math; I guess it never will"—take your impressions seriously.

At the same time, recognize an honest opinion when it's given. There is a difference between the negativism of a discouraged, worn-out teacher, or a teacher with no faith in the learning capacity of the hearing-impaired, and the measured observation of an astute professional observer. A totally honest professional opinion is too valuable to dispense with lightly. It's quite different to hear "Your child seems to have difficulty in grasping English word order, perhaps due to late detection and a relative lack of exposure; I think he needs extra tutoring" than to hear "Your child can't learn word order; if I were you I'd stop pushing him." The former is the professional opinion of a concerned, trained observer and should be given the weight it deserves. The latter is an expression of resignation that has no place in a classroom where children must work hard to learn what comes more easily to hearing children.

Does the teacher concentrate heavily on language?

As a lay person, you cannot expect to evaluate the competence of a teacher in the teaching of language. But in observing a class, you can gain a sense of the emphasis the teacher places on good language usage. The clue lies in the extent to which the teacher monitors the children's use of language. If a child uses the wrong verb form, does the teacher correct the child (but without frustrating the effort at communication)? Constant monitoring—always listening hard and deciding whether or not the language is acceptable—is difficult to do. Nevertheless, language learning is the key to educating the deaf, and the best teachers know the importance of constant monitoring.

As in all things, however, a balance must be struck in language monitoring. Some teachers—like some parents—can go overboard in correcting every last detail, every tiny slipup or error. The end result could well be a retreat from language use on the child's part. The teacher must find his or her own balance, demanding good language use while being careful not to interrupt or undermine the child's effort at communicating. In part, the balance is dependent on the teacher-child relationship. If the children know the teacher really cares about them and their ability to use language correctly, they will take to correction more kindly than when the teacher corrects routinely, as a matter of habit or discipline. In your role as observer, it is the balance between correction and letting communication flow that you should look for and assess.

How strongly does the teacher emphasize auditory training?

This question should help you to determine how seriously a teacher takes the potential in residual hearing. A teacher who shows resignation in the face of deafness—"Well, they're deaf, after all, so why teach them to listen?"—simply underestimates the subtlety of the problem and ignores the wide range of disabilities—from mild to profound—that the term "hearing impairment" covers. Therefore, in both oral and total communication programs look for specific activities geared to encourage the development of listening skills. Does the teacher ask the children to respond to specific sounds, to discriminate, for instance, between a drum and a bell when the children's backs are turned? Above all, does the teacher speak distinctly at all times? Determine to your satisfaction that the teacher has respect for the hearing potential—sometimes measured, sometimes not—of many deaf children.

How careful is the teacher about amplification for each child?

Scan the classroom when you do your observation to see if every child is wearing a hearing aid. If you see a child without one, ask the teacher why. The teacher's answer will indicate a lot about his or her attitude toward deafness and sense of responsibility toward the students in the class. Let's look at some sample answers to the question "Why isn't that child wearing an aid?"

*   *   *

"Well, he has one, but it broke yesterday and it's being repaired."

This answer indicates that the teacher is aware that the aid is missing and knows the reason why.

*   *   *

"Hmmm, thanks for mentioning it. Well, they forget sometimes, you know, or try to sneak out of wearing the aids."

A teacher who is unaware that a student's aid is missing is not doing the essential daily check to see that each child's hearing aids are on and functioning, and thus is taking the risk that the maximum amount of sound is failing to reach all the students in the room. It takes only a simple leap to conclude that a teacher with a blasé attitude toward hearing aids would not be stressing auditory training to its fullest. Remember: Every bit of residual hearing can and should be made to function to its maximum usefulness through auditory training. A teacher who minimizes the importance of residual hearing in his or her deaf students is ignoring a significant potential conduit of communication and learning.

*   *   *

"We just can't convince the parents to take the child in for a hearing test."

There is no reason to doubt the truth of such an answer, but when it applies to four or five children in the class, one ought to feel some concern. If in fact the parents are lackadaisical about determining whether their children would benefit from hearing aids, the responsibility falls to the teacher to somehow get the process started. If the parents are unwilling to cooperate, the teacher must find a way of getting proper amplification on the children. This is an extension of the commitment to deliver information in a variety of ways and to make strong use of whatever hearing, if any, each child possesses. As we have shown, this commitment is inherent in both the oralist and total communication approach.

How courteous is the teacher regarding the special conditions created by deafness?

Terrible as it may seem, many deaf adults recall with bitterness the humiliation of being discussed and criticized by teachers as if they hadn't been in the room at all. Too often, teachers take advantage of their students' deafness—or so they believe—by making remarks in the students' presence that they would never dream of making in a classroom of hearing children: "Oh, Carol's never going to progress much further. Her parents started her too late"; or "Nobody understands James. His speech is completely unintelligible"; or, perhaps equally damaging, "You'd never know Alison was deaf if she didn't open her mouth." As an observer in a classroom, you are in a unique position to determine how much respect the teacher has for his or her charges. Furthermore, a teacher who ignores the possibility that the children might be speechreading such remarks or picking up the gist in other ways betrays a lack of faith in the effectiveness of the communication skills being taught. Use the criterion of what would be acceptable in a hearing classroom to judge the appropriateness of the teacher's remarks. Would one feel comfortable making a given remark in the presence of hearing children?

Is the teacher's approach consistent with that of other teachers in the school?

Continuity is a crucial factor in education. Where deaf children are concerned, ensuring consistency, particularly in the mode of communication used, is often problematical, since proponents of the various conflicting modes often feel strongly that their way is the one sure way. It is up to you to determine whether an oral program remains strictly oral from classroom to classroom and on the playground as well. In a total communication program, the problem is even more subtle, since you'll need to assure yourself that your child's new teacher or new aide uses the same sign language or manual English code as the last teacher. The best way to determine this is to ask direct questions. Great gaps in continuity can remain hidden behind a curtain of assumptions and guesses.

THE WORST AND THE BEST

We thought that in concluding this section it might be helpful to return to our interviews with supervisors of elementary school teachers of the deaf. We asked the supervisors to describe the worst and the best classroom situations they ever visited, and we reproduce two of the responses here:

The worst classroom for the deaf I ever visited? Oh, that's easy. It comes to mind in all its awful details, because it was such a terrible class and such a delicate situation. It was in a school in a fairly rural area, about an hour's drive from the nearest city. The children were all in fourth or fifth grade, and came from all parts of two counties. The really tragic part was that the kids had been in the same group with the same teacher for four years, and they had every prospect of remaining with her for several more years.

The heart of the matter rested with the teacher. The room looked okay at first—it was cheery and comfortable. There was lots of material on the walls of various kinds. It wasn't until later that I started seeing—well, you'll understand, as I did, once you understand the teacher's problem.

I could sense a huge gap between students and teacher as soon as I sat down. She just wasn't getting through at all, she wasn't communicating at all. She was talking—it was an oral program—at a level and in a vocabulary that I knew the children couldn't understand. The awful part was that the teacher didn't know she was weak. She had absolutely no self-knowledge at all regarding her effectiveness.

She wasn't trained as a teacher of the deaf. She was a regularly credentialed teacher and a licensed speech pathologist. It seems that she was the closest to a teacher of the deaf that the district could find to fill the job—it wasn't the kind of place that was likely to attract a young prospective teacher.

The teacher seemed to feel comfortable and competent in her role, but she was clearly unqualified to teach language. She had taken a lot of classes but she was a person who couldn't put book learning into practice. She had a lot of good sources, all the right books and so on—but for herself, not for the kids. There was no projector, no film sources.

I watched her teach a reading lesson to a little girl, and the reasons for her ineffectiveness started to become clear. The girl pronounced every word in a sentence—the teacher had taught her to say each word—but without a glimmer of comprehension. The teacher would repeat every word: "Bobby (Bobby) went (went) to (to). . . ." Then she'd ask a question: "Where did Bobby go?" The girl would have no idea, none at all—wouldn't even understand the question, but after a slight pause the teacher would say, "Yes, Bobby went to the store." And the girl, a good speechreader, would repeat, "Bobby went to the store."

For four years the teacher had been answering her own questions, or feeding the answers to the kids, and she had no idea she was doing that. Those kids were four to six years behind where they should have been.

Once I'd been there for a while I started reading some of the things written on the bulletin board. I remember clearly a very long poem. This teacher liked poems. But this long one was probably at a ninth-grade level. It was easy to see that it was inappropriate for every child in the class; none were reading above first-grade level. I found out later that the teacher was really working on that poem with the children, that they'd been reading it aloud for weeks and weeks. She was just getting them to say the words, only to name words. That's all she ever taught those kids to do.

* * *

The best classroom I've visited is one I'm quite familiar with. I think the key to it all is that everything that goes on there fits together. The teacher teaches a science lesson and then uses the vocabulary from the lesson in the language lesson; the words also go on the bulletin board with a picture of the principle being explained, and perhaps there's a living demonstration of the lesson in the science corner.

It would be obvious to any visitor that lots of language is taught in this classroom. Everywhere are things posted on the walls to reinforce language skills. And this teacher is above all a fine language teacher with good communication skills. She listens all the time to the children's speech and studies their writing, and she doesn't let anything slip by. If the child says or writes *sister* but really means *sisters,* the teacher points it out and asks for a repeat. Her corrections are gentle and she's patient, but her standards are high. And her kids really want to perform for her.

One wonderful thing about the classroom is that the teacher's aide is a young hearing-impaired woman. She has some residual hearing and very good communication skills. I remember one incident in which she made use of her own hearing impairment to great effect. Two of the students in the room were very reluctant to wear their hearing aids—they'd leave them home, or break them, or take them off and lose them at school. The teacher was at her wit's end about it, but one day the aide took it upon herself to bring up the subject. She could tell that one of the hard-of-hearing students was missing a lot that she would have heard with her hearing aid on. The teaching aide got furious: "How can you leave home without your aid? You have so much hearing, how can you give it up? I'd never dream of going anywhere without my hearing aid—why, I'd never be able to work here without it!" The teacher's aide was well liked and well respected among the students, and she certainly served as a good model to the young hearing-impaired kids. The day after her outburst, both wayward hearing aids appeared in place on the children who had resisted wearing them. The image of the aide and her success as a deaf person at work seemed to have made a deep impression.

In some ways I'd say that the teacher in this room along with her aide worked *with* the children's deafness rather than trying to drive it away by sheer stubbornness. They acknowledged the specialness of the situation in every new teaching problem and tried to provide solutions to meet the children's needs.

We hope these portraits give you a springboard for making your own assessment of your child's educational environment.

MAINSTREAMING: WHAT IT IS AND HOW IT WORKS

Mainstreaming refers to the process of sending children with disabilities into the mainstream of society by placing them in regular classes—as opposed to special classrooms or special schools—with their nonhandicapped peers. In broaching the subject of mainstreaming, we find ourselves once more entering an arena of debate where feelings run strong. In this section we present an overview of the subject and the distinctive opinions on all sides, but the outcome of it all is perhaps obvious even at this point. As in many of the issues described in this book, the decision as to whether or not to enroll your child in a regular public school, either part- or full-time, is a difficult, subjective one. A system exists to help you acquire the necessary information, analyze the existing options, and obtain the advice and assistance of professionals trained in the field of deafness. But in the final analysis, your family decision will carry the greatest weight.*

---

*Technically, the decision as to the best education for a handicapped child rests with the courts, not the family, as we explain more fully in a later section. Nevertheless, the action that would bring the decision before a court would almost certainly originate with the parents on behalf of the child. Thus, the decision regarding mainstreaming rests squarely on your shoulders.

Public Law 94-142

The concept of mainstreaming grew out of the Education for All Handicapped Children's Act of 1975, also known as Public Law 94-142. This law in turn had its origins in two lawsuits filed on behalf of two different groups of retarded children that claimed the state was failing to provide the free public education these children were entitled to as dependents of taxpayers. In both cases, the court agreed that children with disabilities, who until then had often been excluded by the public education system, were indeed entitled to free public education. In passing the 1975 federal law, PL 94-142, Congress extended the principle behind these decisions to the whole country. The law required the states to make available to all handicapped children education appropriate to their specific needs.

Until the 1975 law was passed, parents of disabled children were on their own when it came to providing their children with an education. Very often, their only options were enrolling their children in expensive private schools or sending the children to public residential institutions. With passage of PL 94-142, Congress opened another option to these families—enrolling their children in public schools in their own home districts, where individualized education plans would be developed and implemented in accordance with the students' specific needs.

The law recognizes the special conditions arising from the various handicaps and tries to meet these conditions by providing the following rights to all handicapped children aged three through twenty-one:

1. Thorough, nondiscriminatory assessment of the nature and degree of the disability.
2. Free education appropriate to the student's need (if private school is deemed appropriate, costs are covered).
3. Placement of the student in the least restrictive environment.
4. Supplementary aids and services to ensure the students' success.

The key to the individualized education plan for each child lies in the third condition: placement of the student in *the least restrictive environment.* The idea behind this phrase is that the child should not be limited in any way beyond the limitations imposed by his or her particular disability—for instance, by being lumped together with other disabled children and provided a curriculum geared to the lowest common denominator. Such an environment would restrict the child as an individual and, by the terms of PL 94-142, would be illegal.

The sticky problem, however, lies in determining what is the appropriate education and the least restrictive environment for each child. Therefore, upon entering the public school system, the child is assessed, with the parent's permission, by the appropriate personnel (for instance, school psychologist, principal, language or speech specialist, special-education resource teacher). Next the parents, teachers, specialists, and the child, too, when old enough, meet to draw up an Individual Education Plan (IEP). The IEP specifies, for example, whether the child will spend part or all of the school day in a regular classroom; part or all in a special-education center or classroom; which activities he or she will take, and whether these will be with regular students under a general-education teacher, individually with a special tutor, or with other disabled students under a special-resource teacher. In short, the IEP specifies the conditions deemed appropriate by the team composed of parents, educational personnel, and, where desirable, the child. When the plan is signed, it serves as a contract for services to be provided by the school system.

Finally, with the appropriate education plan decided upon, placement is recommended. The least restrictive environment might be deemed by the team to be

1. A regular classroom, with the assistance of a specialist trained in teaching children with the particular disability in question.
2. A special-education environment in a regular school.

3. The one determined by a professional assessment service, which would recommend either a special public school facility or a private school.

Where the parent objects to the IEP or to the recommended placement, he or she has the right to appeal to an impartial but knowledgeable examiner and to bring in a specialist to reevaluate the child and the recommendations. Technically, however, the final decision as to what constitutes "the least restrictive environment commensurate with the child's needs" lies with the courts.

Once placement is made, the child's progress and the effectiveness of the IEP are assessed annually, and the plan is revised as necessary. Also, parents can appeal at any time for a reevaluation and teachers can request a reassessment. It is this responsiveness of the system to the parents' requests that makes the parent's monitoring role crucial.

Kinds of Mainstreaming

We end our overview of the machinery of mainstreaming by listing the types of mainstreaming that have sorted themselves out as workable since the system began operating:

Type 1. Complete but unsponsored, unmonitored mainstreaming. The student goes to his or her neighborhood school, attends regular classes with nondisabled peers, and receives no special services whatsoever. Under PL 94-142 this type of mainstreaming is illegal. Basically, it represents the type of unacknowledged mainstreaming that went on before mainstreaming in the public schools was federally mandated. Where public schools accepted disabled students, they did not necessarily provide any support services or special assistance to handicapped children. Nevertheless, parents often chose to send their children to public schools when the schools would accept them rather than send their children off to residential schools or faraway schools requiring long commutes. Also, parents often decided on neighborhood schools so their children would be in school with children they knew. Today many parents decide on mainstreaming for their disabled children for these same reasons.

Type 2. Complete mainstreaming in the regular classroom with the necessary support services to meet the student's special needs. One function of this chapter is to apprise you of those services available to deaf students in the public schools and of your right to see that they are provided and specified in the IEP, the contract for services to be provided by the school.

Type 3. Partial mainstreaming. The student is based in a special room with a special-resource teacher (a specialist in the particular type of disability or in special education) and attends some selected classes or activities in the general-education mainstream.

Type 4. Team teaching by specialists and general education teachers. Both kinds of teachers team up to teach disabled and nondisabled students in a general-education environment.

Type 5. Reverse mainstreaming. Nondisabled students are brought into the special-education environment for selected classes or activities.

Type 6. Selected academic mainstreaming. Disabled students are based in the special-education resource room and go to the regular classroom for a very limited number of academic subjects.

Type 7. Selected nonacademic mainstreaming. Disabled students leave the special-education resource room and go the regular classroom for a very limited number of nonacademic subjects.

Type 8. Nonintegrated special-resource education in a regular classroom. Disabled students remain with the specialist full-time in the special-education resource room, having occasional contact with nondisabled students on the playground or at school assemblies.

Other plans are possible where parents, child, and the educational authorities agree—for instance, half-day mainstreaming, where the child goes to a regular school for half the school day and a special facility providing specific specialized services for the other half.

The Ideal versus Reality

Mainstreaming as described in the preceding sections might seem to be the perfect solution to the difficult social problem of providing the handicapped with the education they deserve. In theory, as one educator pointed out to us, the mainstreaming process is public education at its very best, involving as it does careful professional assessment of individual students, the setting of educational goals, constant monitoring, parent participation, child-parent-teacher interaction and cooperation, an annual review of each student's progress, and a prearranged system for reevaluation. However, what looks good on paper doesn't always work out in reality. For one thing, PL 94-142 applies to children with a wide range of disabilities, but as we have shown repeatedly in this book, deafness carries with it particular communication and language problems that create barriers to ordinary classroom learning. The first step, then, in assessing the mainstreaming option with regard to deaf children is to narrow our focus from the ability of public schools to serve handicapped children in general to their ability to serve deaf children specifically.

In fact, many public school districts are too small or too poor to develop an adequate program for deaf children, and as education budgets grow tighter, the inability to implement the ideal design becomes ever more common. Poor districts or those with very few deaf students can wind up grouping all the deaf children from the district together regardless of age, auditory skills, communication skills, or academic level. Such school systems may not be able to afford enough well-trained personnel fully aware of the special needs of deaf children; nor may they provide the sort of extra classroom services necessary to an education program for the deaf. When contemplating the option of sending your child to school in your district, how can you begin to evaluate the program offered for deaf

students? To help you start, we provide the following checklist to apply to your local program.
A good program needs

1. To be large enough to ensure grouping by age, hearing level, grade level, and skills level rather than the grouping of all deaf children.
2. Qualified teachers of the deaf.
3. Knowledgeable supervisors.
4. Appropriate curricula.
5. Supplemental services as needed by the students to ensure that they actually receive the education provided.
6. Extracurricular activities in which deaf students can participate.
7. Vocational counseling and training especially designed for deaf students (in higher grades).
8. Appropriate instructional equipment—amplification, captioned films, overhead projectors, and so on.

Support Services
The matter of supplementary support services is particularly important. Too often parents feel that as long as there is someone around who can use sign language or, in the case of oralists, who can reinforce a child's oral-aural skills, their deaf children will be fine in the public school. But the teacher who uses sign language might be just learning; the teacher welcoming the oral deaf student might be inattentive in the classroom. You must make sure that the school provides the support services necessary to ensure that the education being offered actually crosses the barrier of deafness and is received by the child. The child is entitled by federal law to whatever services are necessary to accomplish this goal.
The primary service is that of a special-resource teacher trained in the teaching of deaf students. There are various ways of making such a teacher available to deaf students in a

public school. Some schools maintain a special-resource room for deaf students or for all disabled students, staffed by one or more special-education teachers. The students spend more or less time in the room depending on their Individual Educational Plans, and the resource teachers work with the general-education teachers, sometimes sharing classwork as in team teaching, sometimes simply consulting with the regular teachers as needed. Other districts maintain a single hearing center for hearing-impaired students in the district, which mainstreamed students use as a base, going on to regular schools as recommended by the assessment team. In schools with no resource room or hearing center, itinerant resource teachers visit on a regular basis to consult with regular teachers and work with and monitor the progress of deaf students. Generally, schools near or in metropolitan areas—those likely to have the greatest number of deaf students—provide more special attention than those in outlying or rural areas. Schools with low budgets and few deaf students have fewer resources and may be considered "restrictive" for deaf children for that reason alone.

The services of the special teacher of the deaf is of crucial importance to the mainstreamed youngster. Regular classroom teachers need help in understanding deafness, let alone in applying communication techniques that will be effective with deaf students. We have noted how poorly understood by the general population is the deaf person's relation to language and communication. How can we expect teachers untrained in the special problems of deafness to overcome them when deaf students enter their classes for the first time? The resource person is necessary on campus not only as a teacher and monitor to the child but also as consultant and advisor to general-education teachers, who might be enthusiastic about mainstreaming but completely lost technically.

Some teachers might even fail to realize when they are not getting through to their deaf students and need a trained specialist to help them obtain some feedback. A frequent complaint among general-education teachers is, "But she said she understood! How was I to know she was missing most of what I said?" One specialist told us about a very bright girl mainstreamed in a regular biology class whose teacher conscientiously turned to her after every major point to ask, "Did you understand that, Andrea?" Andrea told her resource teacher, "Well, I always understood when he asked if I understood, so I always said yes. How could I tell him I missed everything else? I couldn't expect him to repeat the whole lesson, could I?" Teachers often forget how hard it is to say "I don't understand" in a room full of people, especially for a child who feels different and whose first concern is acceptance by classmates.

For these reasons, general-education teachers need to spend productive time with specialists in deafness. On the most basic level, a specialist can advise the teachers: "You know, you have a tendency to cover your mouth when you talk"; or "Perhaps you could speak toward the class where Herbie can see you—you speak into the blackboard a lot"; or "I notice that you make eye contact with the interpreter but rarely talk directly to Katy." Such comments alone can go a long way toward successfully integrating a teacher's hearing-impaired students into the regular classroom. Clearly, it is important that you feel that the district offers your child and his or her teachers sufficient contact with trained specialists. Where you feel such services are insufficient, you have good cause to object.

Another important service is that of an interpreter. Many children will enter classrooms where the teacher does not know sign language or is not comprehensible to the oral child. These children are entitled to interpreters, whose services are paid for by the district. In the individual case, you will have to decide whether your child actually benefits from having an interpreter accompanying him or her at school. Some children are self-conscious about being accompanied in class; others, because they understand so much more, are delighted by the service. Furthermore, it is important to determine whether child *and* teacher are making proper use of the interpreter. Often, the student begins relying on the interpreter as a teacher and the teacher gets into the bad habit of addressing the interpreter rather than the student. It's well worth the trouble to take an hour or so to meet with the student, interpreter, teacher, and perhaps the class as a whole in a session designed to help everyone get the most from the interpreter's services.

Another important service, especially for children in the higher grades mainstreaming in regular lecture classes, is that of a note taker. Deaf students are unable to read lips or sign language and take notes simultaneously. Sometimes note takers are friends who agree to take notes in carbon copies; sometimes they are fellow students paid by the school district. One experienced mainstreamed student alerts us to the fact that the best students are not always the best note takers. Very often the average students who must work hard to keep up take the best notes.

Tutors to help deaf students keep up with the work in a regular class provide another possible service. However, if students need a great deal of extra tutoring merely to "tread water" and are barely keeping pace with the class, a reassessment of the educational plan may be necessary. The point of mainstreaming, after all, is to make the appropriate education available in the least restrictive environment. Hours and hours of special tutoring in addition to regular classroom work might well be considered by some to be significantly restrictive.

Other services available and often necessary to round out special students' full access to the education their parents' tax dollars buy are speech therapists, audiologists, psychological counselors, and vocational counselors. In considering the option of enrolling your child in a public school, one of your first steps should be to prepare yourself to request such services on behalf of your child where they are not already available.

MAINSTREAMING: THE DEBATE

With the design of the mainstreaming system clear in our minds, we can begin to examine the pros and cons of the matter. As is not true for many of the debated issues discussed in this book, most informed people believe that deciding either to mainstream a deaf child or to send the child to a special school for the deaf represents a compromise—or perhaps trade-off is the more accurate word. Either way, one must be prepared to give up some benefits and accept some changes. Early in the process it is the parent who makes this trade-off on behalf of the child; later, when the child's opinions are well developed and based on the options at hand, his or her choice will determine the course of action to a large degree.

Let us take a step closer to the more subjective side of the mainstreaming question by outlining the arguments for and against mainstreaming deaf children specifically.

Pros

Many of the pros relate strictly to social adjustment and cultural adaptation. Until the last decade or so, these matters were considered outside the realm of deaf education. Teaching the deaf was thought of as basically a technical problem of transmitting information, and especially language, to children in nonauditory ways. In recent years, however, as the whole culture has begun to acknowledge the importance of the feeling and interacting side of life, concern for the developing self-image and self-esteem of deaf children has gained importance in training courses for teachers of the deaf. In some ways, although PL 94-142 functions to secure handicapped children their rights to an education, supporters of the law see its effects as benefiting the handicapped socially and psychologically rather than academically. The chief arguments for mainstreaming deaf students are the following:

1. Since deaf and hearing people are more alike than different, segregating them exaggerates the difference and distorts both the self-image of the deaf and the understanding of deafness on the part of the hearing. Mainstreaming gives both groups the opportunity to view deafness realistically

and to learn to relate to each other across the barrier of impaired hearing.

2. The self-images of deaf children whose self-perception is based on comparison with hearing children rather than with deaf children alone are stronger and less likely to be focused on deafness.

3. Deaf children in school with hearing children have more exposure to functioning language—as opposed to language presented formally in lessons—and thus more opportunities for imitation.

4. Deaf children in public schools have a greater opportunity to explore the full range of their abilities, instead of having to focus on communication alone, and less chance to reinforce undesirable traits associated with being part of a special group defined by a disability.

5. Parents have a better perspective of the child's skills and abilities than they would if the child were being compared solely with other deaf children in a segregated group.

6. Children in public schools have more exposure to the full range of academic subjects and extracurricular activities. As more deaf children are mainstreamed, one theory goes, the day and residential schools for the deaf become geared to low-functioning deaf children. (Note: this is a *theory* only. Your own research alone, based on your personal observations and intensive interviews with school personnel, will enable you to evaluate the quality of special schools accessible to you.)

Cons

The arguments against mainstreaming follow:

1. The stress of competing with hearing children academically is too great for deaf children, even for exceptionally bright children.

2. The task of learning from teachers not trained to communi-

cate with deaf students is too difficult to enable deaf children to learn well.

3. The risk of social isolation is too great, given the harshness handicapped people often meet with in society at large and the intolerance children and adolescents often exhibit toward those who are "different."

4. Deaf children feel more comfortable with deaf than with hearing peers and do better academically, socially, and psychologically in a learning environment in which they feel at home and relaxed.

5. Deaf children require more intensive, more continuous language training than the public schools can be expected to provide.

6. Most schools are ill equipped and insufficiently staffed to provide the special services promised in the mainstreaming plan.

7. The full burden of mainstreaming falls on the shoulders of general-education teachers. These teachers are already overworked. Their classrooms are too overcrowded to allow them to give individualized attention to regular students, let alone to students with a range of disabilities including communication difficulties. General-education teachers are untrained for the job of teaching special students and are often unwilling to take on the burden. Aside from the extra work involved, they sometimes feel that the presence of deaf students or students with other disabilities will slow down the pace of the class, bring down class achievement, and for these reasons elicit complaints from regular students and their parents.

The Individual Case

Most educators and parents who have had experience with mainstreaming agree on a few important points regardless of how they personally would decide the question. First and most important, they concur that success in mainstreaming is very much an individual matter—in short, it depends on the child.

A good candidate for partial to total mainstreaming would be a sociable child with good communication skills whose success at school could be predicted to outweigh potential failures. There is, of course, no foolproof way of predicting academic success, especially where so many factors—social, psychological, academic, communicative—are at work. Nevertheless, there is some urgency right from the start at making the correct decision, since children taken out of a program might conceivably feel responsible for letting their parents down.

To guard against such a response, parents might treat the mainstreaming option as a great experiment, allowing even the very young child to understand that his or her feelings on the matter have as much weight—perhaps more—than anyone else's involved. As we have indicated, the child's participation in designing the IEP is written into the law, though this participation is invited at the discretion of the parents and educational personnel on the assessment team. Many people involved with deafness believe that for too long hearing parents and teachers have been making decisions for deaf children without taking into account the children's own feelings and opinions. True, an informed adult has a greater capacity than a child for looking ahead and assessing the implications of present decisions for the future. In doing so, however, adults have been known to ignore relevant information right in front of them. Such was the case with Laura's parents, both professional people who had great faith that their daughter's intelligence would carry her through public school despite her deafness.

Laura had always been an all-A student. She spent the first eight years of her schooling in a private oral day school program for the deaf and began total mainstreaming in the ninth grade. Her academic performance remained outstanding after the change. However, by the tenth grade Laura was showing lots of nervous symptoms and was diagnosed as having ulcers. Though her adjustment at the public high school seemed complete, she missed her deaf friends, yearned to be with them, and wanted only to transfer to the school for the deaf that many of her old classmates attended. Her ulcers signaled the intensity of the unhappiness she was feeling.

Laura's parents were violently opposed to the transfer. They were superstitious about the state deaf school and feared that Laura's academic performance would plummet, that she would become a social butterfly but one trapped forever in the deaf world, and that she would lose her incentive to go to college. Laura argued that she'd never give up college—that she wanted to be an architect and that nothing would change her mind about that. She felt her parents were prejudiced against deaf people and that they therefore rejected a part of her own identity. A hiatus in the family conflict was reached when another deaf girl came to the public school when Laura reached the eleventh grade. The two became friends and graduated together. Laura finally resolved her problems by doing her undergraduate work at Gallaudet College, joining many of her old school-for-the-deaf classmates there.

The story of Jason, on the other hand, is practically the opposite of Laura's. His parents had always been serenely unconcerned about the quality of Jason's education, taking the attitude that "everything would work out." Miraculously, it did, perhaps because Jason's older, hearing sister was a voracious reader and disciplined student and served as a role model for the younger deaf boy. Jason went to a regular nursery school and then on to his neighborhood school from age five, and under the eyes of an itinerant teacher of the deaf as well as some enthusiastic general-education teachers, he read and read and read. In the first grade, on the advice of the itinerant special teacher, he was enrolled in a total communication program for half of each day, and in the third grade he agreed to use the services of a sign-language interpreter in class. Jason had his nose in a book from the time he learned to read. He would have chosen to read rather than play on the playground, make friends with his classmates, or engage in extracurricular activities. By the sixth grade, Jason showed no signs of wanting to be anywhere other than where he was.

Despite differences in their attitudes toward school, both Laura and Jason had a firm grasp of the language and did well academically. Intellectual excellence, however, is no prerequisite for mainstreaming. In a partial mainstreaming program, for example, a student could spend periods devoted to visually oriented activities—for example, art, or even arithmetic—in the regular classroom while pursuing the more language-based studies in the special classroom, assuming that a suitable facility was accessible. Thus, the design of the IEP results from a creative use of the available facilities and personnel to match the specific needs and capabilities of the student. Where a creative solution appears to you that others might not perceive, pursue it. Where it is possible and deemed appropriate and least restrictive, an original solution should be welcomed with enthusiasm.

In the context of special cases and programs designed to suit individuals, a word is necessary about the special situation of the hard-of-hearing student in the regular classroom. Very often, children with moderate hearing losses that are compensated to a great degree by hearing aids are sent to regular schools from the beginning and, because of their apparent ability to adapt socially, are given no special attention or help. Parents and teachers too often judge a child on appearances alone, assuming that the known hearing loss causes the child no trouble beyond the relatively slight inconvenience of wearing the aid. The story of Alice demonstrates how harmful such an assumption can be.

Alice's hearing loss was centered in the upper frequencies of sound. She learned to speak with no apparent trouble and was always a sociable and well-adjusted girl, in school and out. However, her high-frequency loss caused her to be deaf to all "s" sounds, "s" being the highest frequency of all speech sounds. The loss might seem negligible to the outsider, and in fact Alice was extremely bright at guessing the meaning of spoken messages from their context. But by missing the "s" sound she missed all plurals ("The girl*s* will explain"), possessives ("the green one is John*'s*"), and important forms of the verb *to be* ("There's no business like show business"; "That's entertainment!"). Consequently, Alice's language skills were significantly underdeveloped, and she lacked self-confidence about expressing herself in writing. Her schoolwork suffered as a result of her poor language skills, but because of her good social adaptation and good speech her poor showing in school was ascribed to a lack of aptitude rather than to her hearing impairment. The fact that she was in a regular school taught by general-education teachers untrained in screening out possible hearing problems masked the problem throughout Alice's school career.

Alice's story underscores what is both mainstreaming's main advantage and, when not properly implemented, its greatest weakness—the constant monitoring necessary of a child's work in light of his or her disability. In this case, by more actively identifying Alice to the educational authorities as a hearing-impaired child, the girl's parents could have assured a more careful screening and the necessary adjustment in added services and special attention.

Early Schooling

Another proposition generally agreed upon is that early schooling—from age three on—is often a factor in successful mainstreaming. The minicontroversy involving early schooling, however, is whether a deaf child is better off in a regular nursery or preschool or in a special day school nursery for hearing-impaired preschoolers staffed by specialists. Proponents of regular preschools argue that a deaf child who begins to socialize with hearing children early will gain a great deal from contact with hearing children. For a start, hearing preschoolers accept deaf children's hearing aids more easily than even kindergartners or first-graders, and generally, in their innocence, accept most differences after an initial question or two. Thus, hearing-impaired children can begin their school lives in an environment of acceptance rather than with a built-in sense of being somehow different from the world "outside."

Those who favor the special school argue that the deaf child's need for intensive training in language and communication skills—in speechreading, speech, or signing—is critical from the moment deafness is discovered, and that preschool is the time the foundations for these skills can be laid down. No amount of communication from hearing peers, they claim, will give language to the child who hasn't been actively instructed in its existence and its purpose.

Regardless of what type of program you decide on—and to a large degree your decision will rest on the relative quality of the various facilities in your area—we urge you to consider enrolling your child in a preschool program as early as possible, preferably as soon as the child becomes eligible. A preschool or nursery program can benefit you and your family in many ways, not the least of which lies in giving you and your child several hours a day apart from each other. You have your life to attend to and perhaps other children who might be suffering from the amount of parental attention and energy their young disabled sibling demands. An ideal schedule would have your deaf child in preschool while siblings were at home, giving the other children the opportunity to spend time with you alone. Even when this schedule proves a bit too good to be true, you cannot help but profit from the time apart from your child to focus on your personal concerns.

Furthermore, as we stressed in the preceding chapter, though you are perhaps a language provider you are not a teacher—nor an arts and crafts counselor, nor a music instructor. A preschool program offers all such personnel plus exposure to more other children daily than you could engineer in your home for your child in a year. Preschool is fun and stimulating for young children and, as we have seen, very young deaf children are in need of nothing so much as stimulation.

An advantage on the side of the special day school nursery program for deaf preschoolers, besides beginning specialized training in oral-aural or total communication skills, is that such schools always have some sort of parent program that enables parents to meet and talk. As discussed earlier, the benefits to be gained merely from sharing one's experiences and discovering one is not alone are enormous.

On the other hand, for the deaf child in a regular preschool, the advantage is a gradual realization that he or she *is* in fact different, *is* unable to participate in certain activities without special help in making adaptations. How much less painful is this gradual acknowledgment than the shock of leaving a loving household at age five and entering a regular kindergarten to discover in oneself for the first time a differentness, an apartness undreamed of and unexpected?

A word or two is necessary here, not, for once, about difficulties to be expected, but about the relative ease with which some deaf children sail through the early years of school. Some children who are used to school from an early age mainstream into regular kindergarten and first-grade classrooms with no apparent difficulty. General-education teachers report such children's adjustment and rapid progress through the curriculum with surprise and delight. The danger for parents lies in becoming lulled into believing that, after the stormy first years, all will be smooth from now on. Such parents are taken by surprise when the child starts slowing down, having trouble in school, and even disliking school for the first time. This often occurs in second or third grade when schoolwork becomes more fully dependent on reading and language. At this point, the deaf child's need to be taught each word and each language construct may well make special tutoring necessary. It is to detect just such changes in the child's performance that reassessment is built into the mainstreaming plan. The program must remain flexible as the curriculum changes and as other factors, the child's development among them, come into play. Simultaneously, parents, student, and school personnel must all be prepared to recognize when a change is necessary and to view it as a natural adjustment rather than a defeat.

Stresses and Strains

Mainstreaming is viewed by some parents as a panacea. "Once my child is in public school with the neighborhood kids," they think, "where he can put his oral skills to work— or take along an interpreter and teach his classmates to sign— everything will be fine." For many families, sending a child away to a residential school or on a daily commute of fifty or sixty miles is simply unthinkable, either for financial or emotional reasons, and mainstreaming in a nearby public school does indeed seem the best solution.

As we have seen, where sufficient facilities and personnel are available and are used creatively, mainstreaming affords deaf students a good education. But an important factor in the jigsaw puzzle is a strong sense of self-esteem and social worth on the part of the child. Without such inner security, the risk is a kind of isolation that perhaps only the deaf can experience.

Consider Karen's story. Karen never developed good communication skills, though through the third grade she went to a special school with a total communication program where, in addition to signing, she developed exceptionally good oral skills. Karen was an excellent lipreader in the classroom and her speech was good but she was extremely self-conscious about using it. When she was mainstreamed into her neighborhood elementary school in the fourth grade, she suffered continually from self-consciousness. Reluctant to draw attention to herself, she refused to consider using a interpreter at school. There was one other deaf student at the school, but he was outgoing, comfortable with his peers, and even something of a school "character"—too popular for Karen to ally herself with. Within a year, Karen was the school outcast. The other children began by making fun of her hearing aids and soon took to jeering at her on the playground. Some sympathetic girls in the class made overtures of friendship, but they rarely approached her singly, instead overwhelming her as a group. The difficulty in communicating and Karen's painfully obvious discomfort soon discouraged them.

Not surprisingly, Karen did failing work in her studies. She missed much of what the teacher said in class and relied heavily on her reading, which was at least a grade level below the norm. The teacher, on the other hand, seemed unaware of the reasons for Karen's poor performance. She simply graded Karen's work and handed it back with that of the others, perhaps unwilling to reach out to one so difficult to make contact with. Or perhaps ignoring Karen was the teacher's way of punishing her for being there at all. With thirty-four children in her class and a new curriculum to teach, the teacher was anything but pleased to find a deaf child in her room.

An itinerant teacher of the deaf visited Karen's school once a week and early on arranged for a special tutor, but it took her two years to understand fully the extent of Karen's isolation. By then the girl had completely withdrawn socially and was barely hanging on academically. Karen's parents were shocked when they learned the truth about Karen's experience in school. They knew she was having trouble with her schoolwork but hoped the tutor would help. Through her whole ordeal, Karen was careful to reassure her parents, to give them the impression of a quiet but happy girl. The actual treatment she received humiliated her so much she was unable to admit to them how awful it was. Worst of all—and completing the circle of Karen's loneliness—the communication between her parents and herself was inadequate for conveying the full picture even if she had wanted to. Karen's oral skills were good at the special school, but they were not sophisticated enough to progress without family support and continual practice. In her loneliness, Karen's speech and speechreading deteriorated.

Karen's story is extreme but not uncommon. A lot of *shoulds* come to mind when one hears the story—the teacher should have talked with the class about deafness, the itinerant teacher should have been alert for the kind of isolation Karen was experiencing, her parents should have sensed something was very wrong. Above all, the assessment team—the teachers, parents, principal, and school nurse—should have been more responsive to the situation. As it happened, however, all meetings were perfunctory, all decisions routine. Everyone involved saw what he or she wanted to see, and Karen suffered two years of utter loneliness—despite all the "shoulds."

Perhaps above all Karen's story underscores the necessity for parents to see themselves as their child's advocates in securing an education. Without you to be aggressive enough to find out what's really going on in school, the child might not have anyone else to depend upon. The worst consequence of such a situation is that the child feels responsibility and guilt for failing and letting down hopeful parents.

How can you tell if your child is doing well in school? One big warning comes first: if you sense an unwillingness on the part of the teacher to accept your child fully into the class, pursue the matter until you are either reassured about the teacher or have succeeded in having the child transferred. Many teachers *are* enthusiastic about teaching mainstreamed children—are willing to make the effort to integrate them into the classroom, to consult with specialists for guidance, and to work with the other students to increase their understanding of deafness. It is these teachers the system must rely on, but you and your child together can serve as an effective means of screening out unwilling teachers who could seriously damage the mainstreaming effort—and your child's sense of purpose— by failing to communicate acceptance.

When placement is made, grow alert to possible signs of stress. Is the child enjoying school—not happy all the time, but happy more often than not and relaxed about going? Does the child share with you things that go on in class, not necessarily when prompted—after all, most kids answer "Nothing" to the question "What did you do at school today?"—but voluntarily? Does the child refer to the teacher as *my* teacher, to the other children as *my* friends? In short, does the child convey a sense of possession and social participation apart from his or her academic work? The implication isn't that the child must be playing all the time or making friends with everyone

in the room. You aren't monitoring for perfect social adjustment, nor should you become alarmed when difficult or
stormy patches occur. Rather, you are guarding against a specific kind of estrangement—the isolation that occurs when
communication fails. Consider fairly—does your child have
sufficient resilience in the face of embarrassment and insensi-
tivity and a real instinct toward and talent for sociability to
shield him or her against isolation? Without these qualities,
mainstreaming may not be the answer, at least not yet. The
child without inner security may need more time in a special
environment to build self-assurance.

Take a lesson from Karen regarding academic stress as well.
Evaluate your child's willingness to go to school and be part of
the program. Consider that a lot of "I'm sick today" or "Do I
have to go?"—especially after a change in the program—
might mean that the child is unable to say directly, "This
room is too hard for me, I don't like it." Remember that mainstreaming is a trade-off, and that special attention from a classroom teacher is sacrificed for social integration and increased
exposure to more subjects and activities. The special-resource
teacher, with perhaps five or six children in a well-designed environment, may have been able to guide your child through every step in the curriculum, but the general-education teacher
in a full classroom will be lucky to meet each student's mini-
mal needs. Again, try to judge fairly your child's need for individual attention and be alert to long downward swings in
academic progress.

Let us end our account not with Karen's sad story but with
the story of Peter, which reflects the best of the mainstreaming
experience and the possibilities it offers. Peter mainstreamed
as a freshman into a public high school from a private residential oral school for the deaf. Always bright, curious, and extremely sociable, he had plenty of exposure to the hearing
world by way of his two older brothers, who drew him into
their activities whenever he came home on holiday or for an
extended school vacation. When Peter moved home for good,

his brothers wholeheartedly helped him with his schoolwork, often making games of the lessons at the dinner table. The whole family had a lively intellectual life and Peter's work and progress at school was of real, not just routine, interest to everyone. Nevertheless, Peter had his problems. He was the only deaf student at the school, and most of his teachers, though willing to help, were unsure of how they should act. Slowly, Peter's diligence and good nature helped them relax. He found his own note takers, made it clear to his teachers where he needed to sit to see them clearly, and talked freely with both students and teachers about the special conditions of deafness and how they affected his studies. For Peter's own self-esteem the final boost came when he was appointed photographer for the school yearbook. He gained recognition and respect from his fellow students not as a deaf person but as a talented photographer, and it was in this capacity that he was able to leave his mark on the school.

Peter did well all through high school both academically and socially, and after graduation chose to mainstream himself into a large university. He selected a campus that offered a full range of services for the deaf. With his old determination, he did admirably there, too, although he met with many difficulties in college that he hadn't faced before, most of them growing out of the complexity of the work. Thus, mainstreaming worked for Peter because Peter himself had the means to make it work. The result was a broadening of horizons to encompass not just the limited options often seen as the destiny of the deaf but the choices open to any person with the capacity to reach beyond a closed circle.

THE INFORMED CONSUMER

Once more, we have tried to look at all sides of a multifaceted situation. Basically, mainstreaming represents a balance reached among many factors, but the X factor, the unknown, is, as ever, your child. You know the child best, and until he or she is old enough to express personal opinions reliably and forthrightly, your voice will speak for the child in deciding the course of schooling. Your role as advocate will be expected and welcomed by school personnel. In the realm of education, you are the consumer who must objectively assess all options to assure that your child receives the best, most thorough, and most suitable education possible. Too often, merely taking what is offered is not enough.

In the near future, your role as a consumer of public education for the handicapped, with full support services and specially designed programs, could be tested even further. At present, the fate of the federal funds that affect mainstreaming and other services for the handicapped are in question. Without sufficient funding, even well-designed programs could falter. We urge you to become aware of the decisions affecting these federal funds and to take appropriate action on behalf of your own children to ensure that the progress toward understanding and social integration of the handicapped is not lost.

Chapter 7

Moving Toward Independence

THROUGHOUT HISTORY, deaf people have been discriminated against and judged falsely. It is not uncommon for deeply ingrained prejudices against deaf people to seep even into households where deaf children are being raised lovingly and with sensitivity. Today these prejudices are less overt than in the past, but they still exist among hearing people, taking their toll on the self-esteem and self-images of deaf children and on the goals these children set for themselves. This chapter is designed to help families combat prejudices within themselves so they can aid their children in developing a strong sense of identity without a built-in inferiority complex, in becoming independent without relying on hearing people for reassurance and support, and in living fulfilling lives without blaming others for the difficulties they must overcome along the way.

In a sense, this chapter is an extended exercise in maintaining a positive attitude. This may seem simplistic, but it is extremely important. Prejudices against deaf people include the damaging beliefs that deaf people are less intelligent than hearing people, that they are less logical, less creative, less suited to academic study, that they have more difficulties making decisions and fulfilling their ambitions. Traditionally, these false beliefs have been accepted by deaf and hearing people alike. As a result, deaf people in our society have been given greater freedom to fail than hearing people. In this context, recall Robert, whose parents, otherwise very strict with their children, subtly undermined their deaf son's ambition to be a veterinarian. In a thousand subtle ways within the home and without, deaf people, like other people with physical disabilities that have nothing to do with their abilities to learn and think, are exposed to the idea that they are less capable, less intelligent, less serious, more emotional, more dependent, and even less important than hearing people. Thus, deaf adults very often choose jobs or careers that are relatively undemanding, limiting their goals to "deaf jobs," which are often characterized solely by manual work, and automatically excluding themselves from more intellectually oriented professions.

It is appropriate to repeat here that deafness is a serious disability with severe consequences involving communication. Denying the seriousness of the problem can be a form of denying the reality of the deafness itself. But as more and more members of the deaf community are proving, an excellent language-oriented education can go a long way toward enabling a deaf person to overcome the communication difficulties related to deafness. Slowly deaf college students are becoming more commonplace, and deaf professionals are to be found in every field. Granted, succeeding in more demanding fields takes considerably more work from a deaf person than a hearing person, and many deaf people *are* better suited for less ambitious work, just as many hearing people are. The point is that all paths must remain open. To close them by suggesting that a child is automatically excluded owing to deafness is to be influenced by attitudes that have their roots in ignorance.

In our world, the characteristic most closely associated with success and maturity is independence. The prejudices and negative social pressures that work against deaf people's success do so by reinforcing their reliance on others. In this chapter, we focus on the myriad ways in which deaf people and their families can counteract the negative influences born of prejudice and ignorance.

OVERPROTECTIVENESS

At this point we leave the protective atmosphere of the home and the relative security of the classroom and step with our children into the outside world. Preparing children to leave the nest, nudging them out on their own by adding responsibilities and freedoms as they become ready for them, make up the natural course of parenthood. But for parents of children with disabilities, nudging children into independence has always presented special problems. The urge is strong to protect such children from discouragement, failure, and even a full understanding of their physical limitations.

This same urge often prevents parents from seeing ways in which their children can function without them. A typical example is the mother who dresses her four-year-old deaf son every morning even though her hearing daughter has been choosing her clothes and putting them on since she turned three. With a bit of reflection, this mother would realize that deafness has nothing to do with the ability to get dressed in the morning, but the habit of overseeing, directing, and helping the deaf child can interfere with even a parent's understanding of deafness.

When it comes to venturing with the child outside the home, the urge to protect becomes even stronger. Safety considerations breed caution, and with good reason—one must somehow alert young children to the approaching cars, warning shouts, and other auditory cues they cannot hear. Research has shown that mothers of deaf children tend to be more anxious, intrusive, and controlling in their relations with their children than mothers of hearing children. (Typically, fathers' behavior is rarely documented, a fact that in itself reflects society's distorted stereotype of the "normal" family.)

The urge to overprotect is understandable when we consider

that traditionally the world has been less than welcoming to disabled people. Like all others who in some way or another are "different" from the norm, handicapped people throughout history have met with intolerance and a serious lack of understanding. Deaf people have had special problems of this type, since fully understanding the consequences of deafness takes some special thought and, often, education. Even the most sensitive people, if they have not considered deafness in great depth, can fail to comprehend the consequences of prelingual deafness for language acquisition and the effects of those consequences on other aspects of life. Not until a person understands the complexities of language and the role of incidental learning in a hearing child's language acquisition can he or she begin to appreciate the difficulty a deaf child faces in learning to comprehend language, to speak, to speechread, to read, and to write.

Thus, it is easy for a hearing person who has not thought deeply about deafness and communication to consider deafness an inconvenience rather than a serious disability and to expect a deaf person to be able to compensate fully and with relative ease for the hearing loss through reading, writing, and speechreading. "Well, too bad deaf people can't hear music, but at least they can see. I'd rather be deaf than blind" is a typical remark. It is worthwhile to remember that Helen Keller would have chosen blindness over deafness. Blindness cut her off from things, she said, but deafness locked her away from people, and this was the greater loss.

Hearing people commonly believe that deaf people can compensate fully for their disability simply by lipreading, rarely appreciating how difficult lipreading is. In fact, this skill is significantly easier for the hearing than the deaf, since hearing people have the complete familiarity with the language necessary for providing contextual information as clues to what is being said.

One more factor contributing to the hearing world's lack of understanding is that deafness is an "invisible" disability. That is, a deaf person does not appear to be disabled, whereas blind or crippled people give some advance warning of their disabilities in the form of visual clues. Deaf people can "pass" for hearing people until they are involved in communicating. Thus, hearing people are often startled and even frightened by a deaf person's speech, so different, as a rule, from normal speech, or by a deaf person's use of signs or written messages.

Parents strive naturally to protect their deaf children from the pain and embarrassment of inspiring shock or fear. But it is only by leaving the protected circle of home and school that deaf children will be able to make use of the society and the culture, an opportunity that is as much their due as anyone else's. Like all parents, parents of the deaf must overcome the urge to protect and must raise their deaf children to understand two things simultaneously: their own value as people and the nature of their disability. Here again we return to the significance of self-esteem and its special importance for children who are "different." To a great extent, the chances of deaf children to succeed and feel at ease in the world at large depend on their ability to take the initiative in communicating with hearing people. To do so they must know themselves well and value themselves highly enough to state forthrightly, in whatever mode they use, "I am deaf," without feeling diminished.

MODELS

The single most important factor in counteracting in deaf children negative societal attitudes is exposure to other deaf people, particularly older people who have achieved independence and some success in their chosen fields. Children need heroes, and deaf children have long been deprived of their own special ones. Until recently, it was not uncommon for deaf children *or* their parents never to see a deaf adult. Deaf teachers often had trouble getting jobs, since many administrators believed that their "deaf speech" or their use of sign language made them poor influences on deaf children. The value of enabling deaf children to see a deaf adult teaching with skill and authority was apparently considered less important than providing strong hearing models. Now, however, as the deaf community becomes more active and as parents become more aggressive in meeting each other and learning about deafness, in most good-size communities it is possible for parents of deaf children to meet deaf people of all ages.

We cannot stress enough the importance of bringing deaf children into contact with deaf people in various walks of life, showing them by example that they are not alone and that their hearing impairment need not limit their aspirations. Deaf college students, teachers, artists, doctors, dentists, athletes, dancers—in a world that often seems bent on limiting the possibilities open to people with disabilities, let your child explore the opportunities open to him or her. Join clubs, go to meetings, invite people into your home.

Your child will not be alone in benefiting from meeting other deaf people. All the members of your family will gain an ease with deafness as they become more familiar with it. One teacher we talked with told us of the strategy she took when she discovered that her junior high deaf students, mainstreamed into a public school, were forming a clique. They refused to associate with hearing students during snack and lunch breaks and refused to sign among themselves, because they felt self-conscious.

That's when I started the sign-and-song program—our kids went to clubs and community groups around the country, signing and dancing to music. We got so popular we were performing two nights every weekend, and the self-esteem of those kids just soared. But it wasn't just because the Kiwanis Club folks liked them that they began to feel good about themselves. It was because their parents and brothers and sisters went to the performances and were really proud of what they saw the kids do. The parents started thinking of their children as artists. They'd sit in the back and hear other parents, parents of hearing kids, whispering, "That's a beautiful thing those kids do. I wish my child could do something like that," and they just puffed out with pride for their children. That was a case of teaching "You are deaf, you will always be deaf; take pride in what you are and what you can do."

Along these same lines, for some people theater of the deaf can be particularly effective in breaking down the barriers between deaf and hearing people and in demonstrating to both deaf and hearing the special capabilities of the deaf. What possibilities might open up to the deaf child struggling to become expressive who sees for the first time a deaf theater performance? On stage are mimes, signers, dancers, or actors making use of the full range of expressive tools, and not just for utilitarian purposes but to highlight the beauty of these tools. Both for deaf children and their families, such a performance could represent a real breakthrough in the full acceptance of deafness.

LEARNING THE WAYS OF THE WORLD

To become independent and at ease in the world, deaf children need what all children need: constant exposure to and instruction in the ways of the world. The difference, as we have noted many times throughout this book, is that where a deaf child is concerned, nothing is free—that is, we must actively teach our deaf children all they need to know rather than relying on the endless capacity for incidental learning that hearing children have. One mother of two sons, one hearing and one deaf, described the difference to us using the most run-of-the-mill example she could think of:

Well, I never had to explain to David, my hearing boy, why he shouldn't swing on the freezer door. Somehow by the age of four he'd picked up the explanations himself. There really are a lot of reasons: the door could break; the meat could defrost and then spoil and then make us sick; the rest of the food in the refrigerator could spoil if the door stayed open too long.... There's no better lesson in the interconnection of all things than explaining the world to a child. For a deaf child like Jonah, who doesn't have the chance to overhear others talk or to pick up something from TV or radio, every fact, every connection, has to be made explicit.

And how much there is to tell! Children need to be told what restaurants are and how they work, what money is, what banks do, how stores operate, where food and clothes come from, what checks are, what tow trucks are, what doctors do. This does not mean that parents should be standing behind an imaginary podium every minute of their waking lives, explaining and teaching all the time. But it is useful to remember that the reasons for performing the actions of everyday life and the meaning of those actions are not self-evident to young children. Simply by remaining aware of your deaf child's need for explicit explanations, you will be closer to meeting them.

So often in this book we find ourselves pointing out the obvious. It bears noting here that the special needs of disabled people, especially of young disabled children, are often overlooked in the busy, workaday world, particularly in families with many children, where life can take on a frantic pace. Many oral deaf adults, looking back on their childhoods, recall that at least one member of their immediate families habitually forgot to face them when speaking to enable them to speechread. On reflection, how obvious it seems that one must face a deaf child attempting to read one's lips, bringing one's face down to the level of the child's eyes rather than towering above and forcing the child to peer upward at an awkward angle. Similarly, it seems to go without saying that one should stand away from a brightly lit window when speaking or signing so a child depending on sight to communicate needn't squint into the glare. And yet people forget all the time. Even in a sensitive, loving home atmosphere, these obvious courtesies are often overlooked. The same holds true for the need to make everyday procedures clear.

The world will grow more predictable to the child who

grows used to the ways of the world. We want our deaf children to feel comfortable and confident about going into a restaurant or a bank and ordering a meal from a hearing waiter or obtaining a withdrawal from a hearing teller. This doesn't mean a deaf teenager on his or her own in these situations has to educate the waiter or teller about deafness. The teenager has only to be able to complete the transaction without awkwardness or embarrassment. One who has been in such circumstances countless times, who has had the transactions explained thoroughly by a parent, and who knows the vocabulary of the particular situation—"Deposit or withdrawal?" "Sign for your cash, please" or "What would you like to drink?" "Coffee now or later?"—will have a greater chance of completing the transaction smoothly than one who hasn't had the benefit of this sort of coaching.

Of course, very often it is necessary for deaf people to make it clear in business or public situations that they are hearing impaired. Although one of our stated goals in this chapter is to point the way toward raising children who are freely able to introduce themselves as deaf people, many of our deaf interviewees felt that hearing people are much less intimidated by "I have a hearing problem" or "I am hard of hearing" than by the announcement "I am deaf." Perhaps you will find yourself and your child in situations where such euphemisms would be useful. When hearing people are frightened or nervous, the rule of "whatever works" to ease the tension seems appropriate.

GOOD NEWS FROM OUTSIDE

In recent decades, society's attitudes about disabilities have begun to change, as they have for all minority groups. Slowly the society has come to realize that it can and should meet the special needs of individuals different from the norm. One important change was the Rehabilitation Act of 1973, which protected people against exclusion from federally funded programs solely because of their handicaps. Another positive change came in 1975, in the form of Public Law 94-142, the Education for All Handicapped Children Act. With the passage of this law, the government formally acknowledged that special efforts were necessary to provide to handicapped people the education guaranteed to all citizens. But the law itself is only one expression of a movement to enable disabled people to mainstream into the society. The deaf community itself has had a large hand in effecting this change. Organizations of disabled citizens are taking it upon themselves to inform the society and legislators about their special needs. The result has been an increase in services available to people with various disabilities, particularly in large metropolitan areas.

To us, this new sensitivity to disability in society represents a steady increase in the understanding and acceptance of deafness. It is our hope that this book will join with other efforts to encourage the growth of independence and creativity in many deaf children.

Appendix

This appendix surveys the kinds of deafness-related equipment and services available to a greater or lesser degree depending on the size of the community. This material should give you a sense of direction as you consider the world your child will encounter outside the home and classroom. Many of the topics mentioned, especially among the services offered, are aimed at deaf adults rather than children. But we have chosen to include this information here not only to point out that such resources do exist but also to help you to educate your child to make use of them as the needs arise.

WHERE THE HOME MEETS THE OUTSIDE WORLD

Snug and private as you might feel at home, the outside world constantly intrudes. The doorbell rings or someone knocks on the door. The telephone rings. An unidentifiable rustle causes you to stop what you are doing and look up. You cannot supply this undercurrent of sounds and signals to a deaf person, but you can equip your home with a number of devices that will translate sound signals into visual or tangible ones. As a result, the deaf member of your household will be able to respond to signals from the outside world without relying on you. Of course, when the deaf person is a very young child, such signalers would be more of a courtesy than an aid to self-reliance, but accustoming a child to the existence and significance of a doorbell, a telephone bell, or a smoke alarm has its own value in familiarizing him or her with the world.

Although the devices described below might seem unobjectionable, it is important to mention that some people have reservations about them. Where auditory training is being stressed in a child's education, signaling devices can be seen as interfering with the child's potential for hearing, recognizing, and using auditory signals. For children being taught to develop their residual hearing, the ringing of the telephone and doorbell would serve as unplanned opportunities to use auditory cues. Supporters of auditory training therefore argue that signaling devices undermine children's spontaneous efforts at using their hearing in a practical setting.

A second objection to installing the full range of available devices is their cost. Unless you are handy enough to create your own system, using an extension cord and a lamp or two (it doesn't take much skill but does require an understanding of electricity), each device represents a substantial outlay of money. These devices could of course be accumulated over time, but in some households they will always fall into the category of luxuries, while in others they will be considered necessities.

Signalers

The signalers you create yourself are those that make an ordinary table light flash when the doorbell or phone rings. Both phone and doorbell can be fed into the same light; the observer soon learns to discriminate doorbell from telephone bell by the rhythm of the light flashes. Another kind of signaler, also simple enough to rig up on your own, is a flasher attached to a smoke alarm. Auditory clues become crucial in emergencies, and deaf people are particularly handicapped by their hearing loss at these times. A flashing smoke alarm, assuming that it is designed well and placed effectively enough actually to awaken hearing-impaired sleepers, compensates the deafness to some extent. This device could make the difference for those who want to live on their own but who are nervous about the possibility of remaining unaware of fire warnings.

Often, alarm clocks are only grudgingly appreciated by hearing people, but for deaf people specially adapted alarm clocks can make the difference between complete dependence on housemates for help in waking up on time and self-reliance in keeping to a personal schedule. Three sorts of alarm clocks for the deaf exist: flashing alarm clocks, pillow-vibrating alarm clocks, and bed-vibrating alarm clocks. Parents who want their deaf children to assume responsibility for keeping to their schedules and meeting their responsibilities might consider one of these clocks a necessity.

Baby-cry alerters are of course essential for deaf parents of young children. These voice-responsive transmitters are available as flashers or bed vibrators. Also on the market are timers, important for cooks, meditators, exercisers—in short, anyone who needs to know without clock-watching when a certain period of time has passed.

The most expensive signaling devices are whole systems, which respond to sound per se rather than to electrical impulses from particular sources. Such systems pick up and signal—via a flashing light—baby cries, dog barks, door chimes, doorbells, door knockers, the opening of doors, clock alarms, and telephone rings. Furthermore, with receivers in various rooms, signals can be perceived throughout the house or apartment. Also, transmitter and receivers are portable, making it possible to set up a signaling system anywhere—in a hotel or a friend's house, for instance. But again, these systems are expensive.

No matter how extensive your signal system, if you choose to have one at all, one relatively simple home-furnishing hint, the extensive use of mirrors, can benefit your child immeasurably. Extend your child's field of vision by hanging mirrors in strategic places: for example, opposite doors, so one can see someone entering without turning around; opposite flashing signalers, so one might notice the door or phone alarm while one's back is turned to the signaler; even tipped slightly at the top of the stairs, so one might perceive from the landing someone coming up the stairs.

Remember, too, that much as you would prefer to discourage the practice, your young deaf child is bound to move around the house more at night than a hearing child of the same age. There can be no shouted questions, no emphatic commands to "go to sleep." If the child wakes in the night, he or she will travel. Make things easier for everyone by installing night-lights liberally throughout the house.

Hearing Dogs

Many deaf people are uneasy about relying solely on flashing light signals. With the exception of the very expensive remote-control signal systems, all signal devices rely on electricity and therefore are subject to failure in a power blackout. Further, deep sleepers can remain oblivious to flashing lights and even to vibrating alarms, a serious drawback when the device in question is a smoke or baby-cry alarm.

Recently, a new kind of signaler has become available to the deaf—a living signaler called the hearing dog. Though perhaps not totally foolproof, hearing dogs offer a kind of dependability that no electronic device can have, since it is based on thorough training as well as that particular brand of affection we have come to expect from our canine friends.

Hearing dogs are trained to respond to specific sounds and to guide their masters to the source of those sounds. Masters and dogs are matched during the training, so the prospective owners can specify which sounds the dogs should be trained to respond to. Thus, hearing dogs learn to respond to baby cries, smoke alarms, telephones, knocks at the door, alarm clocks, and noises signaling an intruder. Owners undertake to reinforce training when the dogs become theirs, and report that the dogs pick up even more specialized tasks, such as signaling the whistle of the tea kettle, the buzzer on the clothes dryer and—in two cases, with no direction from the owners at all—an egg timer.

At this writing, many hearing dog programs are in various stages of planning, but few are in full operation. Therefore, only a very few hearing dogs are actually available. The prototypes for the developing programs were created by the San Francisco SPCA and the American Humane Society in Englewood, Colorado. A third program, Hearing Dogs, Inc., is also in Colorado. The dogs trained in these programs are given to qualifying deaf applicants free of charge. Your local humane society is the place to contact for more information.

TELECOMMUNICATION DEVICES

A vast web of communication covers the globe, and potentially at least, all hearing people are connected by it. Every hearing individual with access to a telephone, radio, and television set can be in contact with the outside world day and night. But not until recent decades was the same opportunity available to deaf people. Even today, although numerous telecommunication devices for the deaf (TDDs) exist, access to them is severely limited by their cost. Nevertheless, although all TDDs range from moderately to very expensive, many families conclude that the potential for communication they provide to a deaf household member is worth the expense.

Teletypewriter Communication for the Deaf (TTYs)

TTYs enable deaf people to communicate by telephone. Although they vary greatly in size and design, basically these devices have a typewriter keyboard on which messages are composed and a means of displaying messages received, either a roll of paper or a display window in which lighted letters move across from right to left as the message is typed.

The TTY user places the receiver of the telephone either

onto a molded bed in the device itself or into a coupler that in turn is attached to the device. Each touch of the keys on the keyboard is converted to a sound signal that represents an individual character; the sound signal is transmitted over the telephone to the receiver's TTY and is displayed on the paper or display window as a visual character. Thus, the sounds unavailable to the deaf on a conventional phone are translated into the visual mode to enable communication to take place.

TTYs are available in all shapes and sizes, from the teleprinter, which is a huge console, identical with a teletype machine, that prints out messages on a roll of paper, to the tiny varieties designed to be carried in the pocket and displaying their messages in lighted letters that advance across a small display panel. Other models include standard-typewriter-sized devices that print out messages on rolls of paper two point five inches wide and devices that fit into attachélike cases whose messages appear on a display window thirty-two characters long. Specific brands of TTYs have particular features. The C-Phone enables the sender to transmit long prepared messages that can be composed in advance, ensuring accuracy and saving on the time it would take to type out the message during the call; it also allows for twenty-four-line instant recall, meaning that both parties can review the more immediate portion of a conversation at will rather than read a message that moves across the screen and then disappears forever. Various models also have limited memory functions, so they can be programmed with emergency messages that are transmittable instantly to the fire department or police. Other differences apply to the keyboards—some models, usually the less expensive ones, have flat keyboards whose letters are merely printed on rather than discrete, raised keys like those on a typewriter. Forming messages precisely and accurately is much more difficult on flat boards than on the more standard models.

The many varieties of TTYs available and the wide range of their prices makes thorough and conscientious consumer research essential. But other factors will have bearing on your decision to install a TTY in your home. Most significant, perhaps, is the age of your deaf child and his or her facility with written langauge. Obviously, a TTY is useless before the child can read and write. But a child who has grasped the principles of written language, though he or she still has difficulty with them, might be a prime candidate for a TTY. For the TTY offers users a source of practice with language outside the confines of the classroom. Children who might be intimidated or bored by language lessons in school and who resist reading on their own might gain a sense of ease with the language in spite of themselves through communicating with their friends in after-dinner social phone calls.

A middle-school teacher in a suburban California program for the deaf gained some local fame by incorporating the TTY into the language curriculum in his class. What made the project possible in the first place was the surrounding community's enthusiasm for the TTYs—the Lion's Club raised money to buy a teleprinter for every deaf child in the school's program. The late Grant Grover, head of the deaf education program at Kent Middle School, Kentfield, California, encouraged phone conversations among classmates and asked his students to bring printouts of their exchanges to class for correction. The teacher was thus able to guide his students in developing their expressive skills based on his analysis of their evening exchanges. This innovative teacher also designed lessons that turned the TTYs into teaching machines. He would type out a series of questions on a TTY, coupled not with a telephone but with a cassette recorder, and leave room for students' answers. The students would then take the cassettes home, play the tapes back through the TTY—with the tapes activating their teleprinters into typing out the lesson—and respond to the questions, bringing in their printouts for grading. One offshoot of this idea has been the TTY Pen Pal Club of America (Room 22, Kent Middle School, 250 Stadium Way, Kentfield, California 94904). The pen pals tape their TTY messages and send them off to other schools or individuals, thus forming a communication network while avoiding long-distance rates.

A factor affecting the social advantages is the number of other TTY owners in the area. Obviously, a TTY will only increase your child's potential for social contact if his or her friends also have access to a TTY. If you live in a rural area with few other deaf children around, you may feel that the expense of the machine is unjustified by the use your child will get out of it. However, this same argument might be used to justify the purchase, since a TTY could bridge the gap between deaf peers separated by distance.

Peer-group interaction is only one kind of communication the TTY makes available to deaf users. Most organizations, public interest groups, and businesses associated with the deaf or with disabilities in general now have their own TTYs. Furthermore, federally funded agencies *must* have TTYs to comply with the law in not restricting access to disabled people, and more and more businesses are finding that it is good practice to maintain a TTY number. Thus, a TTY user gains access to the public side of much of the hearing world as well as that of the deaf world. As the society becomes more sensitive to the needs of disabled citizens and more educated to the existence of TDDs, the use of these devices increases in the society at large. At present, in major cities such public agencies as fire departments, police departments, municipal hospitals, city government offices, and public assistance offices, as well as such specialized services as Alcoholics Anonymous, Suicide Prevention, and so on, are beginning to install TTYs to make themselves accessible to hearing- and speech-impaired people. This is not to say that such agencies in *all* population centers are so equipped—far from it. But the trend is catching on, thanks to the lobbying efforts of deaf- and disabled-people's advocacy groups. The first priority of these groups is making emergency services accessible to disabled people, but the overall concern is to make accessible all areas of the society where the installation of a TTY would make possible the communication of all available information of every sort to speech- and hearing-impaired people. And a long-range goal is to make TTYs available free of charge to all deaf people. So far this dream has not been realized, except in California.

Another important concern of such advocacy groups is to convince phone companies that TTY users should be granted reduced telephone rates. Two factors are at issue—(1) the fact that TTY exchanges take considerably longer than spoken conversations, and (2) the fact that many TTY users make an inordinate number of long-distance calls, since they often own TTYs because they are geographically isolated from sizable deaf communities and from organizations meeting specific needs of the deaf.

At the time of this writing, some progress has been made toward reducing phone rates for the deaf in a few states. When we contacted our telephone company in researching this question, the representative pleaded with us to write of the need for self-restraint on the part of TTY users. She cited a pilot program in Fremont, California, in which TTYs were distributed free of charge to households with deaf members. Typically, she said, because the parties were unused to using the telephone, they made long-distance calls with abandon and soon ran up astronomical phone bills. When they were unable to pay, their service was cut off, and the honeymoon with the TTY was over for good. Advocates of deaf people's rights would surely argue that the issue was not deaf people's inability to learn prudent phone use but the nature of TTY communication itself. While this debate goes on, parents might benefit from the phone company's view and teach their children to be careful about long-distance calls—surely not as difficult a lesson as the service representative implied.

Despite the stalemate on phone rates, the telephone companies in the United States have made some special services available to the speech and hearing impaired. These include special TDD/TTY operator services enabling TTY users to make credit card calls, collect calls, person-to-person calls, and other operator-assisted transactions. For information on special services available to TTY users as well as on local vendors, contact Telecommunications for the Deaf, Inc. (TDI), 814 Thayer Avenue, Silver Spring, Maryland 20910. This is the national organization that coordinates the acquisition and distribution of information on telecommunication devices.

The phone company is encouraging TTY users to list themselves as such in the regular phone directory. However, there is an obvious advantage to listing TTY users separately, so one can determine who actually has a TTY without knowing specific names. Certain local groups have made efforts to list TTY users in regional directories. A notable example is the George S. Ladd Chapter of the Telephone Pioneers of America (an association of hearing telephone-company employees), 370 Third Street, Room 142 B, San Francisco, California 94107. The directory this group produces serves northern California only; other groups in other areas of the country are more or less effective in making listings available. The most reliable directory is an annual directory of TDD phone numbers produced by TDI (address above), which also publishes the *GA-SK* newsletter. TDI is a strong organization run by deaf people and is certainly the group to get in touch with about acquiring, repairing, or listing a TTY.

One particularly useful service available to TTY users is the deaf-community information line operating in most major cities. Local groups write and maintain the weekly tapes that make various announcements of interest to the deaf community. Callers call a TTY number and receive the taped message on their devices. Below is a list of the announcements made on Dial-a-News for Oakland, California, week of February 8, 1981, to give you an idea of the service itself as well as the social life in the deaf community of a medium-sized California city.

• An explanation of a breakdown on the phone lines causing a blackout of Dial-a-News for San Francisco

- Scores for wrestling and basketball in a western regional sports match among secondary schools for the deaf
- A for-sale ad for a TTY answering machine
- An announcement that the local utilities company and rapid transit system now have TTY numbers for questions on billing, services, and routes
- An ad for a music therapist with a special interest in the hearing impaired
- An announcement that a sign-language interpreter will interpret Sabbath services at a local synagogue
- The schedule of captioned films to be shown at a local deaf club
- An announcement of a Day of Prayer for the hearing impaired led by a hearing-impaired priest
- An open invitation to a party given by Deaf Self-Help, Inc.
- An announcement of a ski weekend sponsored by the Deaf Skiers and Mountaineers
- A program note for a particular episode of a sit-com TV show giving the date of an episode featuring three deaf actors
- An announcement of an evening with a group of deaf visitors from Sweden, with three interpreters
- An announcement of a sex education workshop
- An apology and explanation by Joyce Lynch, a local newscaster, whose special show, *Newsign 4,* on which she delivered the news in sign language, had been canceled

The last item was of particular interest to us, since we had been attempting to discover why the ten-year-old show, considered one of the best TV programs for the deaf in the country, had been taken off the air. When we called the station, we were shunted from official to official, but no one seemed to know why *Newsign 4* had disappeared. Not until we reached Dial-a-News did we learn that Lynch had resigned in protest when the format of the show was changed. In the new design she was positioned too far from the camera for her signs to be clearly visible. Dial-a-News asked that callers write to the station protesting the loss of their news program. The item represented a particularly appropriate use of the TDD, since it both informed and invited action.

Movies and Television

Captioned films for the deaf began in the 1960s and gradually became extremely popular. Both educational and feature films, usually at least two years old, since they are donated by the motion picture industry after their prime earning period, are available at no cost (except shipping) to groups with a stipulated minimum membership (six, at this writing). This means that you can form groups of deaf children for the purpose of ordering and showing captioned movies. The only expensive part is buying or renting a projector (one local group managed to buy a projector for practically nothing because its sound system was broken). Be warned, however: The captioned films organizations are strict about enforcing their rules concerning what constitutes an eligible group. To avoid complications, write for information before making any plans. For information and catalogs of available films, contact

Captioned Films for the Deaf
624 E. Walnut Street, Suite 223
Indianapolis, Indiana 46204

Captioned Films for the Deaf
Distribution Center
5034 Wisconsin Avenue N.W.
Washington, D.C. 20016

Despite the arguable quality of its programming, television has a major impact in this country, in entertaining, informing, and shaping the daily lives of most American households. Much of what our children learn about the ways of the world they learn from TV. Until recently, deaf people had only visual access to this medium, but several years ago a federally funded caption center in Boston began captioning ABC's evening news program for showing in a late-night slot. In March 1980, NBC, ABC, and PBS began providing programs in a closed-caption system. An adapting device on the television set is necessary to make visible the captions on the closed-caption system. Adaptors are available through Sears's catalog sales (Sears is making the device available to deaf people at cost, about $250 at the time of this writing). Television sets with built-in adapters are also available at a significantly greater cost.

Although the closed-caption system has generated much excitement in the deaf world, many deaf people complain that the language level of the captions is too high, and parents complain that programming appropriate for children is notably slim. We urge parents not to be discouraged by the first complaint but to welcome the high level of the captions as a challenge to their children's developing reading skills. Like the TTY, closed captioning offers deaf children the chance to practice reading and language skills outside the classroom.

As for the second complaint, that this resource is limited by the number of captioned shows appropriate for children, we hope parents who see the value of the system for giving children access to a significant part of the society's culture will write to the National Captioning Institute, Inc. (5203 Leesburg Pike, Falls Church, Virginia 22041) requesting more captioned programs of interest to children.

A special etiquette applies to the closed-caption system that deserves special mention here. It's easy for parents to switch off the captioner because, for instance, they consider the captions to be at too high a language level for their deaf children. But the real value of the closed-caption system is that it has the potential to give deaf children the same access to television that hearing children have. This means that the fair thing is to allow your deaf child the same freedom and the same voice in the decision-making process that hearing children in your family have regarding the shows to be watched. The temptation to edit your deaf child's choices because the captioner can be switched off easily could restrict the child's access to television without your even being aware of this effect.

INTERPRETERS

Interpreters for the deaf serve as communication bridges between deaf and hearing people, much as foreign-language interpreters bridge the gap between people who speak different languages. Their services are used in any situation in which accurate communication is essential and cannot be achieved in other ways. All government agencies are required to make interpreters available in their interactions with deaf clients. Public schools, private schools, and colleges and universities must provide interpreters for their deaf students, and deaf business people often employ interpreters in conducting transactions with hearing people. In California and a few other states, hospitals must employ interpreters and are responsible for keeping lists of interpreters who can be contacted quickly when a deaf patient is admitted. In California, the courts must provide interpreters to deaf litigants and witnesses, and the interpreters who work in court and other legal proceedings need a special certificate earned through special training, since interpreting legal terms is extremely demanding. This certificate represents a progressive step in the interpreter's profession.

Generally, the rationale behind using an interpreter is this: Even when deaf people are highly skilled in oral communication, both hearing and deaf participants can miss or misinterpret information; when such a situation could be costly or result in poor service, an interpreter is used. When sign language is used, an interpreter is necessary as a translator where hearing participants do not know sign language. Often, interpreters interpret for both parties, hearing and deaf, but some deaf people with good speech prefer to speak for themselves, using the interpreter to interpret to them alone. A good example is a well-known deaf dentist who prefers to speak on the phone to his patients if they call, while his assistant, using a device to divert the received phone messages, interprets the caller's message to him.

Expense is often the deciding factor in whether or not an interpreter is to be used in a given situation. Interpreters for the deaf generally charge for their services by the hour. Interpreters certified by the Registry of Interpreters for the Deaf, Inc., a national program that maintains the standards of the profession, charge a maximum rate set by the RID; noncertified interpreters usually charge less.

A full range of interpreting skills exists, matching the particular needs of deaf people. Thus, there are

- oral interpreters, who translate from audible to visible (speechreadable) speech, or from visible to audible speech, or in both directions, and who have the ability to paraphrase audible messages to make them more readable to the deaf participant
- sign language interpreters who translate American Sign Language into English and vice versa
- sign language interpreters who transliterate manually coded English into spoken English and vice versa
- interpreters who can freely translate or transliterate, no matter which mode or which language is used
- interpreters with special training for interpreting in legal settings.

The RID evaluates, tests, and certifies interpreters at all these levels of skill. Interpreter Referral Centers exist in most major cities; these centers maintain listings of the certified interpreters available locally. If there is no Interpreter Referral Center in your area, contact the Registry of Interpreters for the Deaf, Inc., at the state level, or contact the national RID office:

> Registry of Interpreters for the Deaf, Inc.
> 814 Thayer Avenue
> Silver Spring, Maryland 20910

Interpreters offer a solution to the problem of phone communication between hearing and deaf people where both parties are not equipped with a TTY. The etiquette of the
procedures requires the interpreter to call the hearing party
and say, "Hello. This is Janet Jones (the deaf person's name)
speaking to you through an interpreter"; then the interpreter
relays both sides of the conversation, to the hearing participant
in voice and to the deaf participant in sign language or readable speech. This type of double interpreting, which is not restricted to phone conversation, is sometimes referred to as
simultaneous interpreting.

In the code of ethics developed by RID for its certified interpreters, the interpreter pledges to keep all assignment-relat-
ed information strictly confidential, to convey the content and
spirit of all messages, and to refrain from interjecting advice or
personal opinions. In short, interpreters pledge to serve as me-
chanical translators, not individual human beings, for the du-
ration of their assignments. But the fact is that interpreters *are*
human beings, and many deaf people feel uncomfortable using
their services in situations in which they would prefer to maintain their privacy. So deaf people often choose *not* to use interpreters in those situations in which interpreters might
otherwise be very useful because accurate communication is
essential—for example, conferences with doctors, lawyers, or
therapists.

COMMUNITY SERVICES

The types and amounts of services available to deaf people
depend largely on the size of the community and the size of
the deaf population within it. A large array of services—infor-
mational, social, legal, psychological, and recreational—now
exists in many large cities, and we believe that these services
should be offered everywhere. The range spans a number of
domains: some services are the type offered by public social
agencies, others by private social agencies, still others by organizations of groups growing out of the deaf community itself.

You can learn what is offered in your area by consulting the local social agency that coordinates and disseminates information of interest to the deaf community. If you have trouble locating such an agency in your area, contact the Alexander Graham Bell Association or the National Association for the Deaf, listed below. Their local chapters are reliable information sources.

NATIONAL ORGANIZATIONS, AGENCIES, AND SERVICES
Alexander Graham Bell Association for the Deaf (AGBA)
3417 Volta Place N.W.
Washington, D.C. 20007

An organization devoted to oral education of the deaf and composed of deaf people and deaf professionals. AGBA publishes *Volta Review* and *Newsounds*. The association is run mostly by hearing people; the exception is the Oral Deaf Adult Section within the organization. The International Parents Association of the AGBA, an important organization for parents of children in oral programs, has an office at the same address.

National Association of the Deaf (NAD)
814 Thayer Avenue
Silver Spring, Maryland 20910

An organization of deaf people and professionals who believe in total communication. NAD publishes two periodicals, *The Deaf American* and *The Broadcaster,* plus books about deafness. The parents' organization of NAD is International Association of Parents of the Deaf (IAPD). The organization aids parents through a newsletter, *The Endeavor,* as well as through workshops and correspondence.

National Center for Law and the Deaf (NCLD)
7th and Florida Avenue N.E.
Washington, D.C. 20002

A free legal and counseling service for the hearing impaired. NCLD publishes *NCLD Newsletter.*

Directory of Programs and Services of the American Annals
   of the Deaf
5034 Wisconsin Ave., N.W.
Washington D.C. 20016

An annual publication listing by states of educational and rehabilitation programs for deaf children and adults.

*   *   *

New services and devices related to deafness are becoming available all the time. Staying in touch with the National Association for the Deaf or the Alexander Graham Bell Association is a good way to keep well informed on these developments. Both organizations are excellent sources of information on most aspects of deafness, including legal matters, the whereabouts of local service organizations, and distributors and vendors of devices and media for the deaf.

Index

219